WAGON WHEEL KITCHENS

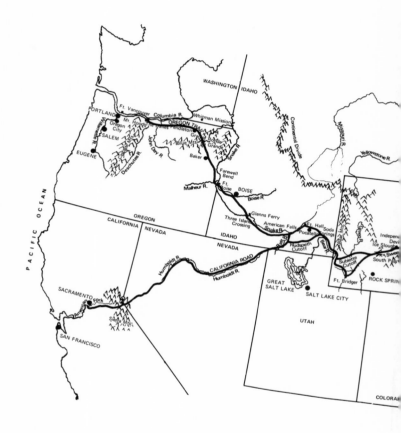

Map of the Oregon-California Trail. Courtesy of Patrice Press, Tucson, Arizona.

MONTANA

WYOMING   WYOMING   S. DAKOTA

CASPER
Red Buttes   N. Platte R.
Ft. Laramie
            SCOTTSBLUFF
        Scotts Bluff
        Chimney Rock
        Courthouse Rock
Laramie   Lower California
            Crossing   Ogallala   North Platte
                                    Kearney
                                    Hastings
                        Ft. Kearny

NEBRASKA

NEBRASKA

OMAHA
Platte R.   COUNCIL BLUFFS
Platte R.

IOWA

S. Platte R.
DENVER   KANSAS

OREGON TR.
Little Blue R.   Little Blue R.
                Alcove Spring   KANSAS CITY
            Kansas R.
                        TOPEKA   Independence
                                    New Santa Fe

Big Blue R.
LINCOLN

Missouri R.

COLUMBIA
Missouri R.
ST. LOUIS

Bents Fort   SANTA FE TRAIL

KANSAS

MISSOURI

NTA FE

N

WAGON WHEEL KITCHENS
Food on the Oregon Trail

JACQUELINE WILLIAMS

Foreword by Sam'l P. Arnold

UNIVERSITY PRESS OF KANSAS

© 1993 by the University Press of Kansas
All rights reserved

Published by the University Press of Kansas (Lawrence, Kansas 66049),
which was organized by the Kansas Board of Regents and is operated
and funded by Emporia State University, Fort Hays State University,
Kansas State University, Pittsburg State University, the University of
Kansas, and Wichita State University

Library of Congress Cataloging-in-Publication Data

Williams, Jacqueline B.
    Wagon wheel kitchens : food on the Oregon trail / Jacqueline
Williams.
        p. cm.
    Includes bibliographical references and index.
    ISBN 0-7006-0609-2 (hardcover) ISBN 0-7006-0610-6 (pbk.)
    1. Cookery—Oregon Trail—History. 2. Frontier and pioneer life—
Oregon Trail. I. Title.
TX715.W724 1993
392'.37'097809034—dc20   93-3233

British Library Cataloguing in Publication Data is available.

Printed in the United States of America
10 9 8 7 6 5 4 3 2 1

For Buddy, who inspired, emboldened, gave hope to, reassured, heartened, and cheered

CONTENTS

ILLUSTRATIONS

FOREWORD

Let's climb on board the history time machine, push the button, and whisk ourselves back to the days of the Oregon Trail. We'll begin the trip by rendezvousing in 1849 at Westport Landing (now part of Kansas City, Missouri) where we've come by steamer from St. Louis.

The steamboat trip itself was an adventure. Broken trees, just underwater, often snagged the steamer and could have punched a hole and even sunk the boat. Rocks and shifting sandbars kept weight-throwers up forward constantly measuring the shallow draft, and there was always the danger the steam boiler might explode in an ugly way. On board, con men and bunco artists swindled the innocent and naive. But excitement was in the air, for the smoke-belching, swish-swish of that stern-wheel steamer on the first stage of "goin' West" gripped everyone's imagination. "Shinin' times" were directly ahead!

Westport was the major staging area for both the Oregon-California and the Santa Fe Trail. But there was a big difference between the two. The Santa Fe Trail was mostly a freighting trail, not heavily peopled with emigrants. The Oregon-California Trail led the "pilgrims" (as the mountain men somewhat derisively called the western-settler emigrants) not only to California but to Oregon and to what later became Washington State. This trail was the main road west, and about 300,000 Americans traveled it from 1840 to 1860. (Can you imagine what a trail of trash that would leave? Historians and western-history buffs are still picking it up.)

What prompted folks to take this difficult trip by wagon? Lots of motives drove the settlers west: a desire for adventure, landowning, or just a new start; the feeling of nothing to lose and everything to gain; bankruptcy; a sheriff somewhere in the East; the lure of the good life.

From Westport, you travel overland. The trip across Kansas and Nebraska seems never to end. The first days on the trail are fun and adventurous. Everybody's on the lookout for the first Indians. Young and old try out their firearms; some travelers get shot by accident. At Ash Hollow (in today's western Nebraska), a small child dies after falling under the heavy steel-tired wheels of a wagon being lowered by ropes down the steep hill to the river valley.

In eastern Wyoming, you anxiously await reaching Fort Laramie, originally a fur-trade fort and now a military post with a well-stocked sutler's store. Here you can trade in your tired and jaded horses for fresh teams. The traders sell you fresh horses fattened up on the lush grass down by the South Platte not far away. Earlier in the summer, these horses, too, had been worn out by their efforts pulling overstocked emigrant wagons and had been traded in by their owners. After a few weeks of grazing, they are ready to be used again.

Fort Laramie is a welcome stop, and in the middle of summer 1849 some 5,000 emigrants per day passed by it. A huge mound of salt pork nearby, jettisoned from the overloaded wagons, doubtless gave the resident coyotes thirsty throats.

The brief stop at Fort Laramie's sutler's store could provide you with a beer, canned oysters and sardines, and even caviar and lobster in the later 1860s. The fort's ovens produced a fine potato bread, and you could restock with potatoes, rice, beans, dried fruits, and even a rhubarb root to keep alive in a small bucket of sand hung from your wagon. And there was ice from the fort's icehouse and some lemon syrup to make a glass of welcome lemonade on a hot, dry-throat summer day. But time's a'wastin'! Saddle up! Move it out!

As you cross Wyoming's prairies, the azure sky lifts the spirits; bumbling big clouds scud by. You can see forever in all directions. It's not like old Pennsylvania, where everything's green, covered with woods, and the roads cut like mouse-races deep through forestland. In contrast, the trail across Wyoming is suntanned and flat . . . and flat . . . and flat.

Woe unto those travelers soaked by the driving rain and lightning storms out in the open prairie of Wyoming. In the heat of July, you suddenly see a huge black cloud racing toward you. The sky darkens and the rain pours in buckets, followed immediately by a bombardment of huge hailstones that rip your canvas wagon-top to shreds and severely bruise you and your companions. Lightning thunders and crashes in your ear as the ground is lit by huge, fat flashes of electric energy. It's all over in fifteen minutes. The heat of summer has disappeared. It's cold. The ground is now icy white, covered for miles with a carpet of hail several inches deep. Makes a prayer-sayin' Christian of you! Scoop some up, add whiskey, and have you a drink! It helps the bruises.

Otherwise the dust is miserable. It wheedles and works its way into every seam of your clothes, your boots, your hair and, mixed with your drying perspiration, makes a crustlike face mask. Horse and ox manure is everywhere. The finely ground, dried droppings from the thousands of animals that have preceded you lift like dust as the wagons in your train cross the prairie. Some folks simply cannot breathe the dust and pull off coughing to drive parallel to the train, away from the dust clouds enveloping the line of wagons. Respiratory ailments are common and are amplified by the manure dust. Face-covering bandannas make the trains look as if they are peopled by bandits.

And you thought you were west when you'd crossed that high open saddle of South Pass in western Wyoming? Guess what? You have the toughest part still ahead. Big mountains, the Sierras, lie ahead, and I mean big! Make tracks before the snows fall in those mountains. Don't get off the road to get lost and die. Stay on the safe route and listen to that ol' mountain man who's leading your train. He knows when the Indians are out there, when to draw in the wagons, how to make a defense, where there's water; pay no attention when he sometimes seems withdrawn and a bit strange. He'll be all right. One more pass to cross.

There it is! The great green-blue Pacific Ocean shimmering out there in the distance. We made it! Now begins our new life. The great adventure lies just ahead.

But what about the nuts and bolts of the trip? Dutch ovens and salt-rising bread, Indian meal and fastnachts, stoves and campfires. In this book, you'll find a fascinating trip-within-the-trip on the great Oregon Trail. Jacqueline Williams is like the old gold prospector who spent years covering great amounts of territory tapping here and there; reading, referencing, and investigating journals, diaries, and historic catalogs; digging constantly into mountains of material just to find a nugget of gold from time to time. And every great once in a while, there'd be a mother-lode pocket of fascinating and detailed information. Such a find makes the chase worthwhile and keeps the prospector ever eager and hopeful. The text that follows is a large collection of the author's nicely polished gold nuggets of historical archaeology. It's a gift to us all.

Sam'l P. Arnold
Food historian

PREFACE

In 1841 the first emigrants to Oregon, the Bidwell-Bartleson party, began their journey; two years later the first large emigrant wagon train left the Midwest for the same destination. In 1849 gold was discovered in California, and thousands of people began the rush to strike it rich. When word was received back in "the states" that the daring adventurers had succeeded, others followed across the prairies and plains.

Many people have told the story of the emigrants' courageous venture to the West Coast. From the jumping-off-towns of Council Bluffs, Iowa, and Independence and St. Joseph, Missouri, the tracks of these overlanders have been followed by scholars eager to examine their route, portray their hardships in the rugged terrain, describe their encounters with Native Americans, or analyze the different roles of men and women. In the search for clues to characterize the great migration west, Sherlock Holmes could not have been more diligent, with one exception: Holmes never discovered what the overlanders had to eat.

In the vast number of scholarly and not-so-scholarly papers and books on the Oregon-California, or Overland, Trail, the way women and men cooked and ate in their white-topped wagons has not been thoroughly investigated. Historians offer laundry lists of categories of food carried in the prairie schooners and perhaps quote an anecdote or two about dried-apple pies and hardtack, but no one has thought it necessary to thoroughly describe those everyday edibles or to wonder about the pickled potatoes overland Margaret Frink prepared. No one has inquired whether "convenience foods" were used or if the "light bread" that emigrants baked was really a special type of bread.

But such questions were of critical importance to the travelers themselves. Was the flour carried a fine white or a type of whole wheat that contained the nutritious bran? Were dried vegetables available? How was bacon preserved so that it lasted several months—or, indeed, did it last? Were the coffee beans preroasted or ground? How did the often burdened-down overlanders make currant jelly or bake pumpkin pies and cookies in the middle of the desolate plains? A focus on the procurement of food and the preparation of meals gives a clearer picture of the daily activities of that period.

When cooks loaded their wagons, they had more to think about than simply packing pounds of flour and sugar. They needed to know if the sugar had to be sifted before it was used, if butter would keep, and if it were possible to make an eggless pudding over an open fire. They had to decide which mill ground the best flour and if the "meat biscuit" publicized in the local newspaper was as good as the advertisement claimed.

Simply surviving the trip was not the only goal. Food was a primary way of providing some pleasure and variety during the endless days of riding and walking. Learning about the foodstuffs contributes to our knowledge of the people who rode the prairie schooners along the Oregon-California Trail and provides another view of mid-nineteenth-century American cooking and eating. As a bonus, a number of minor mysteries about purchases and preparations are solved, and the case is made that American culinary skills were alive and well.

A few statistics show why trail cooking, 1850s style, should be removed from the back burner. In *The Plains Across*, John D. Unruh estimates that between 1840 and 1860, 296,259 people traveled west across the plains. Multiply that number by the amount of provisions recommended by Joel Palmer in *Journal of Travels over the Rocky Mountains*, and simple arithmetic shows that enormous amounts of bread were consumed, copious pieces of bacon were fried, and a massive quantity of apples and peaches (the standard dried fruits) were stewed. Further, if it is figured that 296,259 people each ate three meals a day and if travel time is calculated as five months (it varied between four and six months), one can roughly calculate that 133,316,550 meals were served on the trail. Any event involving such large numbers needs further scrutiny. It is time to examine the culinary record.

In the search for gastronomical clues, travelers' diaries and letters are the first link to understanding the importance of the wagon wheel kitchen. I chose diaries based on information in *Platte River Road Narratives, 1812–1866* by Merrill Mattes and *The Trail West* by John Townley. The former comments briefly on over 2,000 diaries, and the latter catalogs the hundreds of trail journals by subject. Quotations from these diaries are only as exact as I can make them. Generally, rather than the often difficult-to-obtain original manuscripts, I quote from published versions that preserve the original language, including bad spelling and punctuation. Sometimes the diarists' words are exactly as they wrote them, but often the diaries were edited by scholars or even the diarists themselves at a later date. Moreover, to add to the confusion, words and spellings may differ in later editions.

Important as they are, the diaries tell only part of the story. The writer often noted that "we make very good bread & coffee" but neglected to tell what ingredients were used in preparing the bread, what type of flour was available, how the flour was packed and carried, what leavening agent made the bread rise, and how the bread was baked. To answer those questions it was necessary to turn to early newspapers and magazines, books on early mills, and cookery books of the period. When the answers concerning the details of the day-to-day cookery scene are combined with the personal observations of the overlanders, a window is opened to this important part of history.

An advertisement for yeast powder in an 1850s' St. Louis newspaper set me off on a search for a recipe describing yeast powder and led to my finding an early patent for commercial baking powder. When Solomon Carvalho, the official photographer on John Frémont's fifth expedition, described making a dessert with preserved milk, I scanned nineteenth-century magazines and books to discover more about this early convenience food. Trail cooks were among the early users of such new products.

Cecelia Adams and Parthenia Blank, twin sisters traveling to Oregon, wrote that they baked a pumpkin pie but left no clue as to where they found pumpkin. Fresh pumpkin is a fall vegetable usually not available in the summer. Only when I found an advertisement for dried pumpkin in a St. Louis newspaper did I know for certain how it was possible for the sisters to bake a pumpkin pie when they did. Such basic information has been available for years, but no one has ever mixed and kneaded the facts together. It is the combination of diaries and explanations of cooking methods that adequately explains how the emigrants were able to prepare meals day after day for six months.

One reason why this subject has not been adequately addressed before is that often the emigrants themselves thought they "must not write too much about our eating but give an account of other things." After all, everyone knew that people had to eat. Why take up room describing such an ordinary event? Interestingly, many of the detailed recipes are to be found in men's diaries. Possibly because they had not cooked at home, the men thought food preparation was a worthwhile subject to write about.

In this book, I gather the information and the data pertaining to mid-nineteenth-century culinary habits and examine it from the perspective of the people who lived in the prairie schooners. The focus is on the early months of travel, when supplies were adequate and cooks still had the energy to add a dash of creativity to the cookery pot. Chopping, stirring, mixing, and baking were important factors in the settlement of the West, as thousands of men, women, and children benefited from the skills of those cooks who kneaded the dough, stewed the apples, and baked a mess of beans on the arduous journey.

ACKNOWLEDGMENTS

Everyone who writes a history is dependent on the assistance and cooperation of others, and among the many people who supported and guided me in this project, I owe a special thanks to Kathy Mendelson, David Williams, Katie Armitage, and Betty Wason, who read and critiqued early drafts. Their guidance was considerate and critical. Sam Arnold, who loves talking about culinary history as much as I do, gave me confidence to finish; Martha Fulton, registrar at the Museum of History and Industry in Seattle, spent many hours helping me find appropriate cooking utensils to photograph; and Howard Giske did the photographing.

I also appreciate the answers to my many questions and requests from Lynn Anderson, curator at the Washington State Historical Society; Tammis Groft, chief curator, Albany Institute of History and Art; Tony Czech, president of the Midwest Chapter for the Society for the Preservation of Old Mills; Linda Franklin, author of *300 Years of Kitchen Collectibles*; Jacqueline Lewin, curator of history, Saint Joseph Museum; James O'Barr, museum curator at DeSoto National Wildlife Refuge; Don Ofe, site supervisor, Neligh Mills Historic Site; Carla Rickerson, special collections librarian at the University of Washington; Louise Samson, museum specialist, Fort Laramie National Historic Site; Linda Saunto, librarian at the Seattle Public Library; and Jeff Silverman, who made my computer work properly.

Finally, I owe a special thanks to Cynthia Miller of the University Press of Kansas for recognizing that behind my use of the passive voice there was a story to tell.

1

STOCKING UP

Making wise choices among the array of foods available in the mid-nineteenth century was crucial to those adventurous emigrants traveling west on the Oregon-California Trail. Many of the vehicles in a wagon train were filled with foodstuffs since the emigrants did not plan to "live off the land." Although Native Americans and trappers could subsist on the local fauna and flora, it was not realistic for the emigrants to try to do so. They were too unfamiliar with wilderness living and there were too many people traveling the same route to make hunting and gathering the exclusive means of securing food.

Deciding not to rely on the land meant that the overlanders had to transport their own kitchen and pantry. Once they left the jumping-off-places of Independence and St. Joseph, Missouri, and Council Bluffs, Iowa, there would be only a few places for stocking up on staples and fresh produce. "Flour ground at our own grist mill and bacon of home-curing filled the large, four-ox wagon," wrote Catherine Haun.[1] "We have a plentiful supply of provisions, including dried fruits and vegetables, also a quantity of light bread cut in slices and dried for use when it is not convenient to bake," Eliza McAuley recorded in her diary on April 7, 1852, the day she and her family began their journey.[2] Many years later, Phoebe Judson, at age ninety, recalled that at the end of the journey when "all of the little delicacies we brought with us from home were gone, . . . the thought of a 'baked kidney' or 'pink-eyed' potatoes caused the tears to roll down my face."[3]

To learn what to bring and what to leave behind, the emigrants turned to the travelers' guides written by people who had successfully made the trip—even a few who had never left home. Books such as *Journal of Travels over the Rocky Mountains*, by Joel Palmer; *The Emigrants' Guide to Oregon and California*, by Lansford Hastings; *The Emigrants' Guide to California*, by Joseph W. Ware; *Route across the Rocky Mountains*, by Overton Johnson and William H. Winter; and *The Prairie Traveler*, by Randolph B. Marcy gave useful advice about the amounts of provisions and types of cooking utensils to take, how to deal with the Indians, how to cross a river with cattle, and the best routes to follow. The books became best-sellers as an eager public clamored for information about the most desirable and cheapest way west.

For more specific information about the foods to carry and the provisions they might expect to pick up along the way, travelers depended on the letters and journals sent home by people who had completed the trip. The first wave of emigrants who made it to California, the "land of gold," or to the Pacific Northwest were eager to offer assistance. Their pronouncements on "shorts" compared to regular flour, on the benefits of "medicinal brandy," and on coping with dirty water were often printed in the local newspapers. Some would-be travelers considered the advice in letters to be more accurate than that in the guidebooks. The letter writers were, after all, accountable to relatives and friends.

Newspapers printed the letters as a way of encouraging or discouraging overland travel to the West Coast. As might be expected, some editors and politicians thought going west was a superb idea; others felt it bordered on insanity. The battle between them was fought in the editorial pages of newspapers, where each side hoped to influence opinion.[4]

The guidebooks offered a basic inventory of edibles supposed to last the overlanders until they reached sunny California or the rich soil of Oregon Territory. A typical food list would include for each adult:

> two hundred pounds of flour, thirty pounds of pilot bread, seventy-five pounds of bacon, ten pounds of rice, five pounds of coffee, two pounds of tea, twenty-five pounds of sugar, half a bushel of dried beans, one bushel of dried fruit, two pounds of saleratus [baking soda], ten pounds of salt, half a bushel of corn meal; and it is well to have half a bushel of corn, parched and ground; a small keg of vinegar should also be taken.[5]

Although the amounts of foods might change—that is, someone might suggest 150 pounds of flour, others 100—the specific items seldom varied. Nonperishable food was the mainstay of long journeys, whether by land or sea. Without refrigeration or other means for keeping fresh foods cool, travelers had to rely on salted meats, pickled vegetables, dried fruit, bread, and coffee. But within those categories there was variation and choice. Those were the years that saw the expansion of businesses eager to manufacture innovative food products such as meat biscuits and yeast powder. Also, flour mills and sugar refineries turned out more than one product, so emigrants could choose between fine- or coarse-ground flour, brown or crushed sugar.

3

The pioneers purchased their staple foods either at hometown markets or in the jumping-off-places. From a letter written to the *St. Joseph Gazette*, March 6, 1846, and signed "Friend to the Cause," we have a notable record of the activity and the type of merchandise for sale in those early years.

ST. JOSEPH, is situated on the bank of Missouri river, in buchanan county, contains a population of about 1,000 persons, has 13 large mercantile establishments, which are capable of furnishing every article in the *Grocery* and *Dry Good* line that may be required for an outfit, at prices as cheap as the emigrant can bring them from St. Louis.

There is a large Flour Mill, within the limits of the town, besides several others in the neighborhood, that can furnish all the flour and meal requisite, at prices far below what such articles can be brought there.

There is a large Beef and Pork packing establishment there, the enterprising proprietors of which have slaughtered about 250 Beef cattle, and 5,000 Hogs this winter, and are prepared to furnish such articles, either cured in Bacon, or otherwise, as may be needed.[6]

The importance of the food choices that had to be made cannot be overemphasized. At the worst, choosing badly could bring serious illness or death to family members, and if nothing else, picking the right foods and knowing the best methods of preparation made the several-month venture much more pleasant. Today, when supermarkets stay open twenty-four hours a day to provide every food demand, it boggles the mind to think of being

100 or more miles from any kind of store in a slow-moving covered wagon. A look at the bewildering array of food choices that had to be made, and made wisely, follows.

FLOUR: "FIRST RATE"

Baking bread was a necessary daily activity. Flour was such a critical item on the emigrants' list that Nathan Putnam took the time to write his parents in Kentucky: "When you see Stedman tell him that the flour turned out first rate and that when eating it we think of him and wish that we could make him a returne in the hump ribb of Fat Young Bufalo."[7] But what kind of flour was deserving of such praise? We have no idea. And although the letter to the *St. Joseph Gazette* lets us know that mills for grinding grains were available, the writer does not say whether the flour was white, whole wheat, corn, or rye. The flour that Stedman had sent was certainly not the white, bleached flour of today because the chemical-bleaching process did not appear until the early 1900s.

The best source for identifying the kinds of flour was the local newspapers. On March 23, 1850, an advertisement in the *St. Louis Missouri Republican* offered California emigrants kiln-dried flour that "was fully tested and found to be sweet and good after all other flour had soured. It will be put in good and convenient packages." Another ad in that paper from a local grocery store boasted that the store "always had on hand middlings, bran, and shorts" and that their "flour is manufactured from prime wheat, well winnowed and thoroughly cleaned from all impurities." Several stores offered superfine flour in bags. Eagle Mills in St. Joseph guaranteed that their various flours were kept separately.

We have now on hand a large lot of No.1 FAMILY FLOUR, Fine FLOUR & Indian Flour in any quantity our friends may want it. . . . We have also on hand Bran, Shorts, Ship-stuffs and No. 1 Corn meal—But they are not mixed up with our flour, they are all in separate piles. Come and see for your selves. Our flour is warranted, if it is not good bring it back and get your money. We always have flour to sell or exchange with our county friends for good wheat. . . . Don't forget the place, the large Brick Mill.[8]

Catherine Beecher's 1848 book, *A Treatise on Domestic Economy*, defined "shorts" as "the coarser part of wheat bran." Cooks in colonial times equated it with inferior flour; to bring the canaille (or riffraff) home from the mill meant to bring the shorts home. This type of flour was a cross between wheat bran and a very coarse whole-wheat flour—that is, a flour that retained most of the bran and wheat germ but only a small amount of floury material (the endosperm). It was considered a by-product of white flour and was commonly used for livestock feed.[9] Sometimes it was known as "unbolted" flour. In contrast to today's whole-wheat flour that retains the endosperm, bran, and wheat germ and that has all contaminants removed, shorts were dense and coarse and required sifting to remove impurities.

Mid-nineteenth-century mills lacked the machinery to supply clean flour and to remove the bran or the germ from the wheat; improved milling equipment to process flour so that it did not contain specks of the bran and germ was not available until the 1870s. Dirty flour was so troublesome that leading cookery experts implored their followers to learn how to detect impurities in flour. "Good flour adheres slightly to the hand, and if pressed in the hand retains its shape. . . . Dough made of it is a *yellowish white*, and does not stick to the hands after sufficient kneading," advised Mary Cornelius, the author of *The Young Housekeeper's Friend.*[10] Damp flour also caused trouble, and not every mill sold kiln-dried flour. Lucena Parsons complained that "this [airing the flour is] necessary to be done often on this journey or the flour is injured by heating."[11] Too much moisture resulted in a heavy loaf of bread, so the cook had to add extra flour in order to make a dough that was not sticky. Mary Cornelius counseled her readers to notice the brand of flour purchased and if it was good, then by all means to use only that kind. Alas, the emigrants did not have the luxury of such a choice; by the time they determined if the flour was as good as the mill had proclaimed, they were many miles away.

The quality of shorts varied, depending on which mill did the grinding. As early as 1844 Peter Burnett wrote to his family "that what they call shorts are just as good as the finest flour, and will perhaps keep better."[12] Mary Powers concurred and boasted that on the trail she prepared "very good biscuits of shorts without shortening."[13] On the other hand, in winter 1852–1853 while living in Oregon Territory, C. H. Crawford complained that "they had to pay $8.50 for fifty pounds of very poor shorts."[14] Flour that contains large amounts of bran needs extra liquid. Cooks today who bake with whole-wheat flour know that when they adapt traditional white-flour muffin or bread recipes they need to adjust the liquid portion. Some of the emigrants may have discovered this fact sooner than others.

At the same time that the emigrants were rushing to find gold in the West or to make a claim for land in Oregon, the rest of the country was hearing from Sylvester

Graham about the dietary benefits of baking bread with whole-wheat flour. Graham, an ordained minister, was one of the early charismatic food reformers who preached that brown bread was more nutritious than white; graham flour (whole-wheat flour) and graham crackers were named for him. In spite of his efforts, there is no hint of the importance of nutritious flour in the many mill advertisements. At least some emigrants were paying attention to the minister, however, as graham bread was listed on the menu of the elaborate Fourth of July dinner given by the group traveling with E. W. Conyers in 1852. And the transplanted Englishwoman Lucy Cooke, another emigrant, became such a believer in graham bread's nutritional qualities that she wrote to her sister living in Iowa: "We found a sack of graham crackers to day spoiled from damp so we have to throw them away. I wonder if you yet have got any graham flour if not, do there's a dear I'm sure it would be better than white for you."[15]

Middlings, another type of flour available to the overlanders, were coarse and granular and needed further refining to remove the bran and germ. Frequently rye or cornmeal was added to middlings to improve its flavor. The refining process was expensive, however, and the equipment needed to perform this task was crude. Not until 1865 did a device appear that enabled millers to remove the bran from the granular middlings. Many mills offered middlings simply as a cheap flour; going west was expensive, and to those short of money, middlings would have to do for baking the daily bread.

Superfine flour was closest to today's white flour. It was ground between two stones, and then the coarser particles, or bran, were sifted out. By reducing the grain to flour through several grindings and passing the granules through sieves between each grinding, millers obtained an almost white flour. Mid-nineteenth-century cookbook writers such as the popular Eliza Leslie recommended it for cakes and pastry, but she advised her followers to sift or rub the flour through a sieve before using it. In Independence, Missouri, in 1846 superfine flour was available for $2.00 to $2.50 per 100 pounds.

SALERATUS TO MAKE THE BREAD RISE

In order to make their bread and cakes rise the emigrants carefully packed saleratus. Saleratus, from the Latin *salaeratus* (aerated salt), is potassium or sodium bicarbonate, a chalklike substance. It was a commercial leavening product that, like its predecessor pearlash, allowed cooks to bake bread without yeast and cakes without large quantities of beaten eggs. Saleratus had to be mixed with an acidic food or chemical, such as cream of tartar, to activate the leavening process. Unlike our present-day baking soda, which must adhere to a standard formula, the leavening action of saleratus depended on the brand. Manufacturers in that era varied the amounts of chemicals added according to what they thought was the best formula. As a rule, saleratus was stronger than today's baking soda.

Saleratus was first processed by adding carbonic acid to pearlash and changing potassium carbonate to bicarbonate. Later the product was made from the remains of marine plants and sea salt, a fortunate discovery because pearlash was derived from the ashes of trees. Large forests had been stripped to meet the demand for this new product.[16]

Saleratus became available commercially in 1840 and was packaged in paper envelopes with recipes. Catherine

Beecher, considered an authority on domestic matters, advised that "when Pearlash or Saleratus becomes damp, dissolve it in as much water as will just entirely dissolve it, and no more. A tablespoonful of this equals a teaspoonful of the solid. Keep it corked in a junk bottle."[17] Saleratus worked best when added to dough that would bake quickly over a high heat. Cast-iron utensils placed over the intense heat of an outdoor fireplace served perfectly. Cooking over hot coals had many disadvantages but it did produce heat quickly.

If the supply of saleratus brought from home was depleted, the emigrants supplemented it from natural soda springs found near the Sweetwater River. Advised by Joel Palmer that "the water, in many of the springs, is sufficiently strong to raise bread, equally as well as seleratus or yeast," the emigrants looked forward to this phenomenon.[18] Lodisa Frizzell compared the natural saleratus to "frozen snow, forming a crust around the edge of the water." She was not completely satisfied, for "it made [bread] quite light, but gave it a bitter taste."[19]

Amelia Hadley was so intrigued by the large white beds of these soda springs that she "gathered some, and I send you some. It has got durty." She described the beds "as white as snow and this is 3 or 4 inches deep and you can get chunks of salaratus as large as a pint cup just as pure as that you buy."[20] On the other hand, Elizabeth Smith preferred the ready-made variety, complaining that the natural product was "far from being equeal to artificial saleratus although looks as good. . . . It will not foam buter milk one bit." She confessed, however, that she "knew a person to fetch some through and sell it to a merchant for 50 cents per pound not telling him what it was."

Besides using saleratus as a leavening agent in baked goods, Patty Sessions, a famous Mormon midwife who traveled to Utah in 1847, used it to hull corn. Sessions was following the ancient method of removing the hulls from the corn kernels to make hominy (from the Algonquian *rockahomonie*) and samp (from the Narragansett *nasaump*). In fact, that process was one of the first food-preparation techniques the European settlers learned from the Native Americans. The Indians removed the hard outer hull of the corn kernel by soaking it in a mixture of boiling water and wood ash. Sessions, by substituting the saleratus found near Independence Rock for wood ash, obtained the same results. After the hull was removed, the corn was dried and then boiled until soft. If instead Sessions ground the dried corn before cooking it, she served hominy grits to her family.

PRESTON'S YEAST POWDER—NO EXCUSE FOR BAD BREAD

By the early 1850s, a substance called powdered yeast was making its appearance at mercantile establishments catering to emigrants. An advertisement in the July 30, 1851 *St. Joseph Gazette* proclaimed: "Preston's Yeast Powder—No excuse for bad bread—Try them." Yeast powder was also available at the sutler's store at Fort Laramie in 1854 and sold for thirty cents a box.[21]

Yeast powder was the invention of J. P. Preston and J. Warren Merrill, two apothecaries who worked together in Boston; the recipe was patented in 1854. A label found on a can in the cargo of the steamboat *Bertrand*, making its way by river to the Montana mines in 1865, described the yeast powder as

warranted to make light, sweet, and nutritious bread, when good flour is used, and equally adapted to

11

loaves, hot biscuits or rolls, buckwheat and other griddle cakes, gingerbread, and sweet cakes of all kinds. A little added to the batter for fruit dumplings and pot pies will make it elegantly light, and more digestible.[22]

The cans containing yeast powder found in the *Bertrand* after the cargo of the sunken steamer was recovered in 1968 were $3\frac{1}{4}$ inches high by $2\frac{3}{8}$ inches in diameter and made of tin.

Preston and Merrill advertised that their yeast powder "was always READY and SURE to act as soon as mixed." Anticipating that tampering with the product might occur, the advertisement warned, "Do not buy if broken." The directions on the label told how the product was to be used:

To every quart of flour used put two teaspoonfuls of the powder, *and mix them well while dry.* Then mix, as usual, with water, milk and bake at once in a quick oven. To have bread with fine grain it should be well kneaded.

N.B.—*Keep the canister well closed and never dip a wet spoon into it.*

The English gentleman who acquired the yeast powder at the sutler's store at Fort Laramie said he "bought three boxes to improve our bread, as saleratus is poor stuff."[23]

Since the directions do not specify a rising period and advise baking the dough at once, Preston's product clearly was an early baking powder and not actually yeast. This was verified by James Trager in *Food Book* (New York: Grossman, 1970), who credits the first commercially produced baking powder to Preston and Merrill of Boston. Preston and Merrill had the good fortune to be in business after 1835, the year the first tartrate baking powder was developed. That product was a mixture of cream of tartar (potassium acid tartrate), obtained from the residue of wine, and baking soda (sodium bicarbonate of soda).

If one wanted a truly portable yeast and not a type of sourdough starter, it had to be made at home. Eliza Leslie called the mixture patent yeast and included a recipe in her popular cookbook. Portability and convenience seemed to be just as important in the nineteenth century as they are today.

PATENT YEAST

Boil half a pound of fresh hops in four quarts of water, till the liquid is reduced to two quarts. Strain it, and mix in sufficient wheat flour to make a thin batter; adding half a pint of strong fresh yeast (brewer's yeast, if it can be procured). When it is done fermenting, pour it into a pan, and stir in sufficient Indian meal to make a moderately stiff dough. Cover it, and set it in a warm place to rise. When it has become very light, roll it out into a thick sheet, and cut it into little cakes. Spread them out on a dish and let them dry gradually in a cool place where there is no sun. Turn them five or six times a day while drying; and when they are quite dry, put them into paper bags, and keep them in a jar or box closely covered, in a place that is not in the least damp.

When you want the yeast for use, dissolve in a little warm water one or more of the cakes (in proportion to the quantity of bread you intend making), and when it is quite dissolved, stir it hard, thicken it with a little flour, cover it, and place it near the fire to rise before you use it. Then mix it with the flour in the usual manner of preparing bread this is a very convenient way of preserving yeast through the summer, or of conveying it to a distance.[24]

HARDTACK AND CRACKERS

The least-liked food staple made from flour was hardtack, sometimes called "sea biscuit," or "pilot bread." It was a mixture of flour and water rolled into dough one-half inch thick and then baked for a long time in a slow oven. Hardtack may not be tasty, but it keeps for years. When the rains came to the plains, as they often did, hardtack dipped in coffee was frequently the only item on the menu.

John Roger James's family made a batch of hardtack before setting out for Oregon Territory:

Father fixed up a place to mix up a lot of dough and knead it with a lever fastened to the wall. He would put a pile of dough into a kind of trough and would have us boys spend the evening kneading the dough thoroughly, then roll it out and cut it into cracker shape about four inches square and then bake them hard and fill them into seamless grain sacks. There would be no lard or butter used, as there would be danger of them spoiling.[25]

Hardtack had been a staple on long voyages for centuries, and many bakeries in America were set up to manufacture it. The usefulness of this product prompted inventors to design a machine that turned out large quantities of biscuit without sacrificing flavor and durability. According to the description given in *Scientific American*,

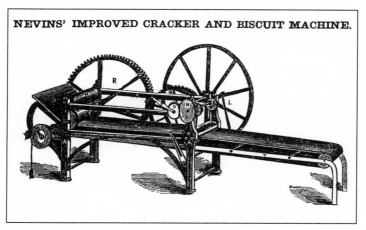

Improved cracker and biscuit machine. Illustration in *Scientific American*, November 13, 1847.

November 13, 1847, if the rollers did not receive the dough properly, the crackers and biscuits were "afterwards apt to split open and in warm latitudes soon spoil." Yet this machine, the writers said, had met even the standards of the British navy.

The bakeries and grocery stores in towns that supplied emigrants were quick to advertise their hard bread as a necessary commodity. "To California and Oregon Emigrants" was boldly written across an advertisement in the *St. Louis Missouri Republican*, April 12, 1850:

J. Noe, Brooks has now on hand one thousand [barrels] best kiln dried hard bread, just baked expressively for California emigrants warranted to keep perfectly good for two years. He is constantly baking the above articles and will be prepared to fill all orders either in boxes or bags.

One hopes that Brooks's hard bread was better than the brand purchased by S. H. Taylor: "The hard bread manufactured at St. Louis or Kanesville [Council Bluffs] . . . is bad—always very bad. I believe nobody eats it except when unavoidable."[26]

Similar to hardtack but lighter because of a leavening agent, crackers appeared at many meals on the trail. Sometimes the meal was a simple one of "plain middling meat, crackers and heavy biscuit," as George Curry described in a letter to the *St. Louis Reveille* in 1846. Other times the meal was more varied, as Ellen Tootle recorded: "Had ham, dried beef, crackers, pickle and syrup for dinner with brandy today."[27] Crackers and hardtack were most appreciated on days when there was not enough time to bake bread or if there was no fuel to start a fire.

Grocery stores and bakeries sold a variety of these biscuits or crackers to many eager emigrants, and some families baked a supply of crackers and packed them in the provision box before starting their journey. Consumers had their choice of Boston biscuits or milk, water, or soda-cracker biscuits. The newly designed cutting machines came on the market just in time to relieve commercial bakers of the laborious task of hand-rolling the dough. Family recipes were fairly simple, but hand-rolling large quantities certainly must have been a chore. Consider this recipe for soda biscuit:

SODA BISCUIT

Take 1 lb. of flour, and mix it with milk enough to make a stiff dough; dissolve in a little milk 1 tea-spoonful of carbonate of soda; add this to the paste, with a tea-spoonful of salt. Work it well together, and roll it out thin; cut it into round biscuits, and bake

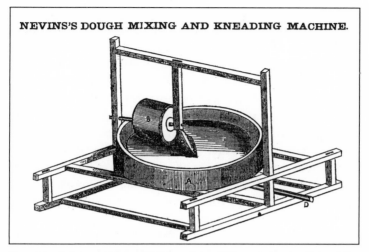

Dough-mixing and kneading machine. Illustration in *Scientific American*, November 13, 1847.

them in a moderate oven. The yolk of an egg is sometimes added.[28]

PARCHED CORN AND CORNMEAL

Parched corn and cornmeal scored high on the list of desirable commodities because they were easy to cook with and did not spoil or turn sour. Several pioneers commented on the culinary attributes of this quintessential American grain. According to Peter Burnett, "cornmeal [would keep] to the mountains, and parched corn meal all the way.... The parched corn is most excellent to make soup."[29] The S. H. Taylors praised it even more: "It is remarkable that all are excessively fond of corn meal in every form in which it is cooked. Every one expresses satisfaction or regret as they happen to have it or not."[30] The

Taylors were less enthusiastic about substitute corn-starch, calling it "a failure, because it requires eggs to make it good." The ingredients that went into substitute cornstarch are another unsolved mystery.

In his guide book, Randolph Marcy called parched corn "cold flour" and favored crushing the corn in a mortar until it had the consistency of coarse meal and then mixing it with water, sugar, and cinnamon so that it becomes "quite palatable." Half a bushel of cold flour is "sufficient to subsist a man thirty days."[31] The name parched corn indicates that the kernels were roasted in an oven or sun-dried. Flint corn was the popular variety grown for cornmeal.

Mush, the porridge made from cornmeal, was an easy food to prepare and was mentioned in many an emigrant's diary as "mush and milk" for supper. It had been popular since colonial times when Americans switched from oatmeal or wheaten porridge to the equivalent dish made from corn. Known as hasty pudding in New England and "suppawn" (from the Narragansett *Nasaump*) in New York State, the Pennsylvania term "mush" became the popular name for this Native American staple.[32] Charles Putnam, dutifully writing to his mother and father, gave his version a four-star recommendation and called it tola: "Tola is the best dish I ever eat, it is made of parched corn ground, & cooked in the same manner that mush is. It is sweetened with sugar."[33] Putnam may have been misspelling "togus," another New England name for a variety of mush. Charles urged his parents to be sure to bring corn when they decided to go west, for "parched Corn Ground into meal and sifted is first rate. . . . It will last ten years." When Putnam, a Kentuckian, made his version of mush, he may have followed the advice of Lettice

Bryan, the popular Kentucky food writer who featured this recipe in *The Kentucky Housewife*:

> Sift some fine Indian meal, make a smooth batter of it by stirring in a sufficiency of cold water. Having ready a pot of boiling water, throw in a handful of salt, and stir in your batter till it is like very thick soup. Boil it till of the proper consistence, and stir it frequently to prevent its being lumpy, and to keep it from burning at the bottom. Mush, made in this manner, will never fail to be thoroughly done and clear of lumps, which are two common failures. Cold mush may be sliced and fried brown in butter. They are very good for breakfast.[34]

SUGAR

Sugar, another item that came packaged in many forms, is usually referred to simply as sugar in guide books, diaries, or letters. Although it was not as important as flour as a survival food, everyone carried it. Pies, cakes, and jams from fresh berries were frequently made on the trail (having a sweet tooth is a common and timeless malady).

Grocers sold sugar in several forms. The advertisement for Berthold and Ewing Grocers in St. Louis, Missouri, in 1846 featured New Orleans and Havana sugar, crushed sugar in boxes, and loaf sugar. Advertisements in St. Joseph, Missouri, newspapers offered molasses in barrels and brown, clarified, crushed, powdered, and loaf sugar.

Sugar in the mid-nineteenth century came from sugar cane imported from Caribbean countries or grown in a few southern states. At the time of the emigrants' journey west, only Louisiana produced large amounts. But in 1847 "the best qualities of loaf crushed and powdered sugars and golden syrups, are made entirely of Cuba sugars. . . . [Only] the medium and common qualities, of refined sugar and sugar-house molasses, are made from Louisiana sugars," reported the *Western Journal*.[35]

Although experiments to produce sugar from sugar beets began in this country as early as 1838, the process did not yield large quantities until the 1870s,[36] long after the emigrants had baked their pies and puddings on their journey west. Sugar came into this country in large cones or loaves and was broken down by the refineries into smaller loaves that were sold in grocery stores. These smaller cones or loaves were molded and resembled pointed hats. Loaf sugar was traditionally wrapped in blue paper, from which the thrifty housewife extracted blue Indigo dye. Merchants displayed the cones by hanging them up with a heavy string or cord that ran vertically through the cone's center. The cones contained a mixture of white and brown sugar, with most of the white on the top. The sugar had to be dried, ground, and sifted to remove impurities before it could be used.[37] Fastidious cooks washed it. Emigrants, of course, could not be bothered with this nicety; water was too precious, and sugar that had been washed needed to be reprocessed into crystalline form. Sugar nippers, a cross between scissors and pliers, were used to break up the cones. Loaf sugar would not have been carried in the provision box because it was difficult to unwrap and pulverize the loaf. It was also heavier than the crushed sugar, a key consideration since the emigrants were sometimes carrying as much as twenty-five pounds of sugar per person.

Until the 1870s, it was expensive to separate white and brown sugar and difficult to remove all the juice, or molasses. Brown sugar was a raw, lumpy, sticky product often called muscovado sugar (from the Spanish *masacabado* or Portuguese *mascavado*, meaning unrefined). It was quite different from today's brown sugar, which is nothing more than white sugar colored with a little refined molasses. As late as 1872 *The New Cyclopaedia of Domestic Economy* still classified brown sugar as an inferior product:

> [I]f you like to pay for dirt, and to mix it with your preserves, puddings, and pastry, and choose to believe that sugar which moistens even thick paper they place it in, and which looks dark, smells strong, and sticks to your fingers, is richer in sweetening than clear sparkling white sugar, out of which none of the sweetening but all of the dirt has been washed—then buy brown sugar.[38]

Because the cheap brown sugar still contained molasses, Peter Decker in his list of staples advised emigrants to consider carrying both brown and crushed sugar. "Brown sugar to last to the S. Pass would answer well—after that the hot sun would make it run, so part of it at least should be crushed sugar."[39] The crushed sugar that the emigrants purchased had more of the molasses removed, but it was not pure white. The grocer had performed the first step for the consumer: The loaf was unwrapped, crushed, and put out for sale. Often, grocery stores had small, portable sugar mills available so that the customer could grind the lumpy substance at the time of purchase—a nice convenience for the busy homemaker.[40] Recipes of the period called for "pounded loaf sugar" or "finely-pounded loaf sugar."

Havana sugar most closely resembled today's white

sugar, and it was recommended for use in cakes and fine pastry. But it too needed extra crushing and sifting. "Have it pulverized by pounding it in a mortar, or crushing it on the pasteboard with the rolling-pin. It should then be sifted," recommended Eliza Leslie.[41]

Most of the overland cooks probably carried the serviceable brown or crushed sugars, which were the cheapest. Indeed, the few writers who considered it necessary to describe the sugar specified brown sugar. Although the overlanders did much baking on the trail, even making pies and cakes, one doubts that anyone had the time to bake fancy cakes or pastry (except on July 4). There was no need to spend the extra money on a fine white sugar, which often cost as much as ten cents per pound more than brown sugar.[42]

In any case, whatever variety was carried, sugar was a sweet and useful commodity that occasionally played a part in solving everyday "infirmities of human temper on a long trip." Bernard Reid, who was traveling with 125 men on the Pioneer Line, a commercial passenger service to California in 1849, captures the spirit of the day:

> For a good while back our rations of sugar had been growing small, and at our frugal board some were given to complain that others were taking more than their share. This led to unpleasant bickering, and to avoid its continuance I proposed to make a little muslin purse or sugar bag for each of the mess, into which the sugar ration was to be equally distributed when served by the commissary every fifth day. Then each man could help himself at meal time out of his own stock, and no one could complain. This was assented to, and I was appointed to spoon out to each man his

equal modicum of sugar. It worked like a charm, and there was no more bickering from that cause.[43]

"BREAD AND BACON, BACON AND BREAD"

Next to bread, bacon was the food most eaten; it often appeared on the menu twice a day. Bacon received mixed reviews. Abigail Jane Scott praised it: "A peice of bacon placed between two peices of bread actually tastes better than the best of cakes and pies at home."[44] George Curry accepted bacon as a fact of life: "Life on the plains far surpasses my expectation. . . . Bacon and hard biscuit may occasionally interfere with his *fairydom*, but that only occurs twice a day, and the influence is but momentary."[45] Helen Carpenter complained that it occurred too often on the menu: "But then one does like a change and about the only change we have from bread and bacon is to bacon and bread."[46] Bread dipped into bacon grease was called hot flour bread.

Eating on the plains, however, was not like eating at home, as Ellen Tootle might have explained. Before her trip Tootle had vowed she would not eat fat meat such as bacon. Yet at a meal of boiled potatoes and fried flitch (a cured and salted side of bacon), Ellen confessed she enjoyed it. Poor Tootle, her appetite cost her a prize. Ellen's husband had bet her a new dress that "before [she] was halfway to Denver" she would eat fat meat. He reminded her of the forgotten wager after she had eaten three pieces of flitch.[47]

In his guidebook, Randolph Marcy not only recommended bacon but advised that "bacon should be packed in strong sacks of a hundred pounds to each; or in very hot climates, put in boxes and surrounded with bran, which in a great measure prevents the fat from melting away."[48] Bacon, because of its high fat content, spoiled readily and was one of the items frequently thrown away. Alonzo Delano graphically described a piece of bacon ready for the trash bin: "We discovered that we had been imposed upon in St. Louis in the purchase of our bacon, for it began to exhibit more signs of life than we had bargained for. It became necessary to scrape and smoke it, in order to get rid of its tendency to walk in insect form."[49]

When stocking up on provisions, the overlanders would purchase bacon at a general store or from a traveling peddler. If they had lived on a farm before their journey, they would have salted and preserved pork for bacon at hog-butchering time. In the mid-nineteenth century, the term bacon included a broad category of the meat from a hog and might refer to sides, hams, or shoulders. It was purchased or preserved as "cured side bacon" and sliced as needed. Good bacon had white fat; if it was streaked with yellow the meat was considered unfit to eat. Saltpeter was used to make the meat red. "Bacon—Hams, sides and shoulder for sale," E. Livermore and Company, a grocer in St. Joseph, Missouri, 1845, advertised.

An early recipe for curing bacon appeared in *Mrs. Hale's New Cook Book*. The emigrants probably had similar recipes since smoking and curing bacon are ancient methods for preserving pork. Mrs. Hale directed her readers to

> cut off the hams and head of a pig, if a large one; take out the chine and leave in the spare-rib, as they will keep in the gravy and prevent the bacon from rusting. Salt it first with common salt, and let it lie for a day on a table that the blood may run from it; then make a brine with a pint of bay-salt, one-quarter peck of

24

common salt, about one-quarter pound of juniper-berries, and some bay-leaves, with as much water as will, when the brine is made, cover the bacon; when the salt is dissolved, and when quite cold, if a new-laid egg will swim in it, the brine may be put on the bacon, which after a week must be rubbed with the following mixture:—Half pound of saltpetre, 2 oz. of sal-prunella, and 1 pound of coarse sugar; after remaining 4 weeks, it may be hung up in a chimney where wood is burned; shavings, with sawdust and a small quantity of turf, may be added to the fire at times.[50]

The proper fuel for smoking the meat seemed just as important as the ingredients for the brine. Several writers in early newspapers listed the type of wood to be used. One called for old wood that had rotted because the wood made large amounts of smoke with little fire; another suggested using a peck of mahogany sawdust for 100 pounds of hams and doing the smoking in a seed cask. The hams were usually smoked for several weeks.

BEANS AND RICE

In 1849 white beans were advertised for sale in the *St. Joseph Gazette*; the "demand was brisk," and the beans sold for forty to fifty cents per bushel. Whether this was the variety of bean that most of the emigrants used for cooking is difficult to know; there were and are many varieties of beans, and the emigrants certainly had their favorites, just as we have today. Old-fashioned beans, such as the cranberry bean and Jacob's cattle bean, may have simmered and stewed at mealtimes as the overlanders traveled on the prairie schooners to the West. The progeny of these older varieties of beans are now considered heirloom seeds.

Joseph Conlin, in his book about the food on the western mining frontier, writes that "on the actual emigration, however, beans were not so conspicuous because they required so much time to prepare."[51] He was probably referring only to baked beans, which do take time, since many diary entries describe the emigrants cooking and eating beans. The apparent contradiction arises because many writers made no distinction between plain simmered beans and the baked variety.

Beans were cooked when the company stopped for the night or when they "nooned," the essential two-to-three-hour break from traveling. "Encamped on a large plane and sat up till about 12'Oclock cooking beans," Charles Gray recorded in his journal.[52] "Most all of the families cooking beans to day," wrote Jane Gould.[53] "We live fine we have Pork & Beans. We started with 20 bushels and you know I can go it on them," Captain De Wolf wrote in a letter to his wife, perhaps with a bit of humor.[54] Mary Black "swaped a large tin of peaches for as many beans and cooked half of them for dinner."[55] She made a wise trade, as cooked beans are loaded with protein, fiber, vitamins, and minerals. Moreover, if the beans were dried, a quantity the size of a can of peaches would certainly have fed more people than the peaches would have.

Since it is just as easy to cook a large quantity of beans as a small amount and since cooked beans would keep several days, the task did not need to be done every day. And it was easy to soak the beans overnight or even while traveling. The only drawback was spilled water; a bumpy ride would not have hurt the beans. The cooks surely followed the example of Cecelia Adams and "cooked beans and meat

... in quantitys sufficient to last some time." The biggest hindrances to bean cookery probably were finding water and trying to cook beans at high altitudes where water boils at a lower temperature and the food needs a longer cooking period. Peter Decker encountered just such a problem when he was crossing the Sierra Nevada Mountains: "Put beans over boiled 2 hours & were yet hard. Ate the soup & left determined not to be detained again by beans that would not cook (a watched kettle dont boil)."[56]

In his journal Charles Gray wrote, "About 10'oclock partook of a supper of baked beans."[57] To save time, water, and precious fuel, generally the beans simply were simmered in water in a Dutch oven rather than baked. "Boiled a big mess of beans, to be warmed over for several meals," noted Catherine Haun, and other travelers talked about cooking or stewing beans.[58] In fact, when William Swain listed beans as part of their Fourth of July dinner, he pointed out that the beans were boiled and baked, which suggests that baked beans were prepared only for special meals.[59]

At mealtime, the cooked beans were heated up with bacon or whatever meat was available. "I had an opportunity at noon to eat some of Mrs. Dobbins' cold beans. The boys cooked so much bacon with them that each bean had a rim of grease around it. Oh well, I can plainly see that I am too particular," Helen Carpenter admitted.[60] The cooking water or "pot liquor" surely was used as a base for soup or for the "hotchpotch" stew that James Hutchings prepared. Emigrant cooks did not waste anything; they were masters at recycling. Mary Hopping came up with perhaps the most creative method of preparation when she "cooked beans to a jelly and formed them into a loaf" that she spread on sandwiches.[61] Since Dutch ovens were on almost every list of desired utensils, cooking beans did not require a special pot.

Baked beans, on the other hand, must first be cooked until they are soft and then require a long, slow cooking time in an oven. Those emigrants traveling without a stove would set the bean crock in the hot coals; a Dutch oven provided the perfect container. But the process would use extra fuel, and there was no nutritious broth left for soup. Beans were baked but not so frequently as they were simmered.

Emigrants did at times gripe and grumble about eating beans. Charles Gray might have "relished [baked beans] with more 'gusto' than any game supper I remember of," but many travelers no doubt agreed with Mary Burrell: "Would feel pretty well myself if I had not eaten so many beans. They make me feel so w——y."[62]

Varieties of beans, *Phaseolus vulgaris* and *Phaseolus lunatus*, such as kidney beans, pinto beans, black beans, and limas, are native to the Americas. They were brought to North America from Mexico, and by A.D. 1,000, Native Americans on the East Coast included beans in their well-developed agricultural system. By the time the European explorers landed at Roanoke Island, North Carolina, in the sixteenth century, beans of "diverse colors" were growing among the corn fields.[63] Since dry beans store well and are easily turned into a cheap, satisfying dish, they became a staple food for travelers.

Rice was another filling, starchy grain that simmered beside the cooked beans or stewed apples. Joel Palmer recommended taking ten pounds of rice per person on the journey west, and in 1846 a letter writer to the *St. Joseph Gazette* suggested allowing fifty pounds of rice for each mess (a party eating together). Charlotte Pengra, who kept a daily diary of foods she cooked, often had rice on the menu. "I have since stopping stewed a pan of apples a boiler of rice" was a recurring entry.[64] Mrs. George Donner ranked rice with beans: "Rice and beans are good articles on the road"; Sallie Hester included rice as one of the foods "we live on"; Lucy Cooke ate a supper "consisting of fish Tomatoes Rice & ham with hot bread & tea";[65] and Helen Carpenter had some rice spiced with verdigris (copper sulfate), which when leeched into foods can be poisonous. Carpenter commented on the rice dish to show that emigrants could eat almost anything. "Only the other day, I saw some rice being warmed over that had been cooked and left standing in the kettle which was brass. There was a rim of verdegris all around the edge. The cooks stirred it in and nobody was even sick from it."[66]

On the other hand, S. H. Taylor gave rice a negative rating. "Rice seems to be less relished on the road than at home—I presume because we have not eggs to cook with it. The emigrant will find that anything usually cooked with eggs, is of little use on the road."[67] And Peter Decker had trouble getting rice cooked properly. "Fine morning left camp at 7 o'clock after our mess partaking of turtle soup made of turtle & rice, the latter not done and scortched, first turtle I ate, meat good & tender."[68]

From the evidence we have, it is likely that the rice was boiled and then added to stews or soups. One might even speculate that Lucy Cooke prepared a fish stew whose delicate aroma scented the surrounding woods or that Charlotte Pengra combined her stewed apples and rice, sprinkled in some dried ginger or nutmeg, added a few nuts, and feasted on rice pudding.

PRESERVING THE FOOD SUPPLY

Salting and pickling were the primary means of preserving fresh meat and produce in the mid-nineteenth century. The canning industry was just getting started and not until after the Civil War would it be equipped to supply large amounts of canned goods throughout the country. At any rate, cans were too heavy to carry in the prairie schooner.

The salt the emigrants purchased could have been American or foreign. Selected companies boasted in newspaper advertisements that they sold Kanawha salt, which came from the Kanawha River in Virginia, indicating that it was American salt and not an import. Other salt-producing areas were in New York, Ohio, Pennsylvania, and Michigan. Not everyone bought American. An advertisement for an imported salt in the *St. Joseph Gazette*, January 30, 1846, stated that "the pork is to be first salted with Turk's Island salt (coarse) and then carefully packed with same article, in pieces not exceeding eight pounds each." But whether imported or domestically produced, lots of salt was recommended for the journey; for example, Palmer suggested that the emigrants carry ten pounds.

Various types of pickles took up room in almost every prairie schooner. Basil Longsworth listed three gallons for his group. Pickles and pickled foods were popular because these foods did not spoil, they added salt and spice to a meal of plain bread and crackers, and most important, many emigrants believed that pickled foods prevented scurvy.

Overlanders knew that fresh fruits and vegetables prevented scurvy, but they did not know why. (Vitamin C was not identified as the necessary ingredient in the prevention of scurvy until 1935.) The emigrants reasoned that if a fresh cucumber or any vegetable did the trick, a pickled one would, too. Unfortunately their assumption proved erroneous. Even pickles made from cucumbers that are high in vitamin C contain only two to three milligrams of vitamin C per pickle as the vitamin is destroyed during the pickling process.

Nevertheless, in 1850 when Margaret Frink and her husband decided to seek gold in California, they were perturbed that no pickles were available at the stores selling supplies in St. Joseph, Missouri. Pickles and pickled foods, such as pickled salmon and pickled herring, were frequently listed in the inventories of grocery stores that advertised in the daily newspapers. Eighteen fifty was a popular year for going to the goldfields of California, however, and stores catering to emigrants often ran short of supplies. In order to obtain the essentials, Frink was sent on the road to try to find them:

> He was fortunate enough to find a bushel [of cucumbers] still in the salt, which he bought and brought back with him. This, with some horseradish and one peck of potatoes, was all he could find in the way of vegetables. I prepared these very carefully, and put them up in kegs with apple vinegar; these were to be our principal defense against that dreadful disease, the scurvy.[69]

By the time of the Civil War, pickled potatoes were sent by physicians' orders to supplement the soldiers' diet of white flour, fat meat, beef, and beans. Perhaps the doctors were influenced by reports from the emigrants. Alas, even though potatoes are high in vitamin C, pickled potatoes, like pickled cucumbers, lose the vitamins. The following recipe for pickled potatoes appeared in an 1869 cookbook (although it came out after the Frinks' trip, Margaret Frink probably used a variation of it, no doubt without adding beetroot to the potatoes):

PICKLED POTATOES

Wash and peel some very early potatoes, cut them into long thin slips, and pass them through two or three waters; drain them upon a cloth, and then sprinkle them with fine salt; let them remain for a half an hour, rub them dry in the cloth, and put them into a cold pickle of spiced vinegar to which a clove of garlic (bruised) or a sliced shallot has been added. If well done, and the potatoes are of the proper kind this pickle is beautifully crisp and will take any flavor communicated to it in the vinegar, such as that derived from a mushroom or two. A few slices of boiled beetroot will give it a fine red color.[70]

Was scurvy a problem for the emigrants? It is hard to know, for there are few accounts of the disease in the emigrants' diaries. Frink, in fact, was one of the few diarists who indicated she was worried about scurvy. Not writing about it, of course, does not mean that no one was thinking about it. After all, the emigrants never mentioned pregnancies in their accounts, yet many babies had their start on the Oregon-California Trail. Still, it is puzzling that so few people alluded to scurvy because they did write about sickness. Diaries are filled with references to people having diarrhea, stomachaches, and toothaches, and the deaths from cholera are recorded as if the writers were making a statistical survey.

DRIED FOODS AND PORTABLE SOUP

In addition to the usual dried fruits, which everyone carried, dried vegetables also showed up in the provision box. Marcy, in his book *Prairie Traveler*, advised his readers to take desiccated or dried vegetables since they had been successfully used by the U.S. Army. Marcy claimed the dried items would keep for years if not exposed to dampness and that they retained their antiscorbutic properties. He was wrong about the latter assertion. (Techniques to preserve the potency of water-soluble vitamins such as vitamin C in dried vegetables were not perfected until 1930.) Marcy included this recipe for the preparation of dried vegetables.

> They are prepared by cutting the fresh vegetables into thin slices and subjecting them to a very powerful press, which removes the juice and leaves a solid cake, which, after having been thoroughly dried in an oven becomes almost as hard as a rock. A small piece of this about half the size of a man's hand, when boiled, swells up so as to fill a vegetable dish, and is sufficient for four men.

Letter writers to newspapers and magazines also advised emigrants to carry dried pumpkins and dried onions. A columnist for the *Scientific American*, March 1, 1851, went so far as to recommend a particular brand:

> Ground, dried pumpkin, an article of merchandise prepared by United Society of Shakers at Harvard, Mass, . . . is the best substitute for the pumpkin "yellow and ripe from the fields," that we know of. Good pumpkin pies may be made at all seasons of the year, by obtaining the pumpkin ingredient as above.

The writer also suggested that when milk was not available for cooking, the cook should substitute crackers and water. Cecelia Adams and Parthenia Blank, twin sisters traveling together to Oregon in 1852, proved that dried pumpkin worked, for they baked pumpkin pies one Sunday while they should have been resting. What a treat that must have been. They do not mention whether the baking was done in a stove or over an open fire.

One of the most intriguing dried foods advertised "to persons crossing the plains" in the 1850s was meat biscuit. This ad appeared March 25, 1853, in the *St. Louis Missouri Republican*:

> Meat Biscuit—This highly nutritious food, patented in the United States and in England by Gail Borden, Jr., having passed the severest ordeal of the great Industrial Fair in London . . . one pound of it contains the nutriment of five pounds of the best fresh beef; one ounce will make a nutritious soup. It will keep in perfect preservation for any length of time. In tight tin cannister or casks. . . . The traveler across the plains can always have a fresh supply of food easily and quickly prepared.

The biscuit was apparently similar to portable soup, which was made by boiling meat or fowl with the bones in a rich broth until the soup was thick, like jelly. This concentrated gelatinous substance was then set in pans or cups and allowed to dry until it was hard and could be broken easily. By adding the dry substance to boiling water, one had an instant soup.

American women often made portable soup, popularly called "soup-in-his-pocket," at home. E. Smith in *The Compleat Housewife* (1742) had written that the tablets "were good for woodsmen against the fluxes which they are very liable to from lying too near the moist ground and guzzling too much cold water." Eliza Leslie, who reportedly "adopted her work for the period," provided instructions for making portable soup for the pioneers setting out for the West.

Further investigation shows that meat biscuit was somewhat different from portable soup, yet both are forerunners of today's bouillon cube. The first steps for preparing meat biscuit were the same as for preparing portable soup—that is, meat was boiled and reduced to a gelatinous substance. But instead of simply drying this jelly, large amounts of flour were mixed in and the final product was baked. The process was perfected by Gail Borden, the man who made condensed milk popular. *Scientific American*, March 8, 1851, printed instructions for making meat biscuit:

> Mr. Borden's soup bread is a different preparation [from portable soup], and he was granted a patent in 1851 for the same. He takes the very best quality of beef which can be found in Texas, and extracts the gelatin from it by low steam heat. This is afterwards—in a state of spissatude—kneaded with flour or any kind of vegetable meat, into cakes, and baked slowly in an oven heated by steam. By using a high heat to extract the gelatin from the meat, a very unpleasant flavor is communicated to it, for the high heat sets a portion of the phosphorus contained in the bones free and gives this an unpleasant odor to the extract. Mr. Borden carefully avoids this—his extract is of as fine a flavor as Liebig's portable soup, and the baking of it into cakes, along with vegetable substances, enables it to be carried with ease over mountain and sea, and tends to preserve it from atmospheric influence, so as to prevent putrefaction. In

Texas beef is very cheap, so are fowls, such as turkeys, chickens, &c. Of this kind of meat, the very best alone is used by Mr. Borden. . . . We have eaten some of Mr. Borden's biscuit, made into soup, and liked it very well; an ounce of it made a good hearty meal. . . . For sea voyages and long overland journeys, we believe it to be a grand compact article of food and the time may come, when it will be found in every house in our land, as a most excellent and cheap basis of our soups.

Portable soup received endorsements from several early explorers. Crossing the Bitterroot Mountains, Meriwether Lewis and William Clark found portable soup invaluable when their other supplies ran out: "We dined & suped on a skant portion of portable soup, a few cannisters of which a little bears oil form our stock of provision."[71] Lewis and Clark had purchased 193 pounds of portable soup in Philadelphia.

John Wyeth considered it indispensable and said the soup was a must for anyone traveling across the continent. "When the second company shall march from the seat of science, Cambridge [Massachusetts], we would advise them to pack up . . . a competent supply of portable soup."[72] Wyeth began his trip in 1832, and although he did not make it to the Pacific Coast, he felt called upon to advise would-be adventurers. S. H. Taylor was surely describing portable soup when he recorded that "flesh of poultry, 'cooked down,' is found an excellent article of food."[73]

Meat biscuit, though not specifically recommended by Capt. John Frémont, was carried on his fifth expedition. Solomon Carvalho, the official expedition photographer, speaks of it several times, once as part of a meal served in Frémont's lodging. "First came the camp kettle, with buffalo soup, thickened with meat-biscuit, our respective tin plates were filled and replenished as often as required." And during the winter, when the Frémont party, like Lewis and Clark, were without food, he reported, "We were on rations of meat-biscuit, and had killed our first horse for food."[74]

Despite the good advertisements and the celebrity testimonies we cannot infer that either portable soup or meat biscuit was popular with the ordinary emigrant. Few diarists and letter writers mentioned either product. Was it because the biscuits were so ordinary, too expensive, not tasty? Or were people simply suspicious of new products? It is true that meat biscuit was commercially available too late to be mentioned in the popular guidebooks, but we know that portable soup was for sale in 1803. Moreover, both portable soup and meat biscuits were lightweight, convenient, and nutritious. With the addition of a few greens or some wild onions, the dried-soup base became a good defense against scurvy.

Coffee cake was another processed dried food in the same category as meat biscuit, that is, an innovative concentrated food touted as a boon to emigrants.

Superior Articles for California Emigrants
Fine coffee cakes, fine tea do [cakes]; fine Lemon do; four pieces a pound. To one twelfth or fifteenth part of a cake give a good cup of coffee, tea or a glass of lemonade. The price is very cheap and the article is packed up in lead, entirely water proof as well as air tight.

From this ad in the *St. Louis Missouri Republican*, April 12, 1850, it sounds as if coffee cake was made from concentrated dried fruit mixed with flour and perhaps baked, like meat biscuit. Unfortunately, no recipe has been found, and unlike meat biscuit and its verifiable superior quality, there seems to be no mention of anyone using coffee cake. Except for the ad in the St. Louis newspaper, the product is absent from accounts of dining on the plains and prairie. But because the ad is so intriguing, I imagine and hope that someone gave it a try.

A CUP OF COFFEE

Although Peter Burnett advised his family, "If you are heavily loaded let the quantity of sugar and coffee be small, as milk is preferable and does not have to be hauled," his counsel was the exception.[75] Most emigrants took the advice of Anna Maria King: "Fetch what coffee, sugar and such things you like, if you should be sick you need them."[76] By the time the travelers were nearing either Oregon or California, coffee was sometimes the only provision left. Leslie Scott, an Oregon pioneer, recalled those times:

> We still had coffee, and, making a huge pot of this fragrant beverage, we gathered round the crackling camp fire—our last in the Cascade Mountains—and, sipping the nectar from rusty cups and eating salal berries gathered during the day, pitied folks who had no coffee.

A story about coffee illustrates the relationship between Ellen Tootle and her husband, newlyweds on their way to Colorado to look over the possibilities of expanding their dry-goods business to Denver:

> Mr. Tootle says I cannot do anything but talk, so would not trust me to make the coffee. Boasted very

American coffee grinder (ca. 1870s). Courtesy of the Antiques Gallery, Seattle, Washington (photographer, Howard Giske).

much of his experience. He decided to make it himself, but came to ask me how much coffee to take, for information, I know, but he insisted, only out of respect. The coffee pot holds over 1 qt.; I told him the quantity of coffee to 1 qt. He took that, filled the coffee pot with water then set it near, but not on the fire. I noticed it did not boil, but said nothing. When they drank it, they both looked rather solemn and only took one or two sips. I thought it was time to have an opinion upon it. As Mr. Tootle would not volunteer one, I inquired how the coffee tasted. He acknowledged it was flat and weak, but insisted I did not give him proper directions. He consented to let me try it at supper time.

Later that evening Ellen Tootle had her chance to prove her culinary skills:

> I was all impatience to try my skill in making coffee. I watched it anxiously until it was boiling and waited with the greatest solicitude and I must acknowledge some misgiving, for them to taste it. Oh, but I was rejoiced and relieved when they pronounced it very good.

Before making a cup of coffee, the green coffee beans had to be roasted in a skillet and then ground in a grinder. The names of the beans indicated their place of origin, and we find Rio, Havana, and Java coffee beans listed for sale in the mid-nineteenth century. If tea was preferred, the buyers chose from a list of brands that featured Gunpowder, Imperial, Young Hyson, Souchong, and Poushchongre.

Not until after the Civil War did manufacturers devise a good way of preserving the flavor of preroasted or ground coffee, sometimes referred to as essence of coffee. But from the March 30, 1850, *St. Louis Missouri Republican* this ad suggests that they certainly tried.

California Outfits
Ground COFFEE—Put up in water-proof and air-tight packages and guaranteed to retain its strength and flavor for years.

The credit for a good roasted coffee goes to Arbuckle Brothers, whose offices were in Pittsburgh, Pennsylvania.

The company patented a method of sealing in the roasted flavor by coating the beans with a mixture of egg white and sugar. Roasted coffee beans in paper bags were then shipped throughout the West, and Arbuckle coffee was the most popular brand.[77]

FOR MEDICINAL PURPOSES

Completing their list of staples and recognizing that there might be stressful situations during the journey west, realistic emigrants included brandy, rum, or whiskey in their inventory of necessary provisions. Drinking was a popular pastime for many Americans. Temperance societies began to organize in order to discourage "the use of ardent spirit and the traffic in it, by example and by kind moral influence" as Americans ventured west.[78] The Washington Temperance Society, the forerunner of Alcoholics Anonymous, was organized in 1840. Between 1846 and 1855 thirteen states and one territory, Minnesota, passed prohibition laws.

Unless they were really opposed to alcohol, "most emigrants take five to ten gallons of whiskey to a wagon under the notion that by mixing it with the bad water it becomes in some mysterious way healthy and purified," according to Addison Crane.[79] It is not exactly clear whether Crane was referring to the water or the whiskey. To make the whiskey go further molasses was added; the popular name for that drink was "skullvarnish."

D. B. Ward and Elizabeth Smith did not make excuses but claimed that alcohol was carried for "medicinal purposes." So did the Tootles, according to Ellen Tootle's diary: "The brandy and whiskey we brought for medicinal purposes, but indulged in a little as we had just started on our journey. The first day, the cork came out of the whiskey bottle and spilled more than half, to Mr. Tootle's great disappointment. Indeed I don't believe he has recovered from it yet."[80]

Charles Gray was so convinced that the medicinal powers of brandy could make people feel better that he "made a divident, each a bottle full of our fine brandy & made some *poonches* which were delicious—like water in the desert to the fainting traveller or the smile & kiss of love! Oh, Lord, how practical these brandy *poonches* are!"[81] One thinks of a punch as being a mixture of fruit juices and alcohol, but it sounds as though Gray's punch was pure brandy.

The idea of alcohol for medicinal purposes had such great merit that the party of E. W. Conyers agreed to adopt it. Conyers described their detailed plan for having a nip now and then.

> Now none of us were in the habit of taking a drink, yet we came to the conclusion that it would benefit us, keep us from taking cold; therefore we were a little sick and took some brandy all around. I want to say right here that we had agreed that no one was to have any brandy from that bottle unless we were sick, and then a little quinine must be added. . . . The brandy seemed to give us instantaneous relief.[82]

And it seems that even the cows recovered when they had a sip. "Had to cross a very bad alkali swamp and had to rush the cattle through to keep them from drinking the water. When they get alkalied the remedy is a good dose of whiskey," reported Eliza McAuley.[83]

For those emigrants who cared to indulge, a wide variety of wines and spirits was available. Native wine, Madeira, rum, Jamaica rum, American gin, Holland gin, American brandy, cognac, champagne, bourbon, scotch, and whiskey were listed for sale in St. Louis and St. Joseph newspapers. According to one merchant the alcohol was sold at wholesale prices and put up in one-, five-, ten-, or twenty-gallon kegs, iron bound. In 1852 a gallon of whiskey cost twenty cents—a cheap price for medicine. Whiskey was the cheapest; hard liquor, brandy, and cognac did cost more.

A LITTLE SOMETHING EXTRA

The basic list of provisions was supplemented by culinary extras that the overlanders brought from home, purchased in the jumping-off-places, or found at trading posts along the way. As best they could, families made every effort to have good food on their long journey, at least in the beginning. By the time the emigrants reached Fort Hall and made the last push to their new homes, the emphasis was more on quantity than on quality.

In 1853 Basil Longsworth added hams, dried beef, dried peppers, tartaric acid, and cheese to Palmer's basic list.[84] Helen Carpenter packed dried herring, a small quantity of cornstarch, a frying pan, and a rolling pin; clearly, she planned to bake pies. She later added sweets to her supplies, paying seventy-five cents for candy.[85]

To replenish her supplies, Jean Baker, an Englishwoman who had traveled up the Mississippi River from New Orleans to St. Louis and was on the way to Salt Lake City, added green vegetables and a whole sheep that she found for sale at the small Mormon town of Macedonia near Kanesville (Council Bluffs), Iowa. The sheep cost one dollar.[86] Unfortunately, Baker did not record what she did

43

with the meat. Was it roasted? Did she make it into jerky? Were the bones used for soup? Did she render grease from the fat?

Another transplanted Englishwoman, Lucy Cooke, took along a supply of chocolate. While her party made a stop at Fort Laramie, her husband bought a can of preserved quinces, two bottles of lemon syrup at $1.25 each, and a packet of candy. Lucy apparently had a sweet tooth, for she often wrote that "I drink chocolate all the time since I've been sick." A cup of hot chocolate would have been a comforting brew. Baker's chocolate and prepared cocoa were available to the overlanders. (Baker's chocolate has been a household name since 1765 when James Baker opened the first American chocolate factory.) Lucy Cooke's family also loaded up with "36 lbs prunes, 2 boxes figs, a lot of raisins, so we shall have some nice thins occasionally." The fruit of course was dried; large amounts of fresh fruit were too heavy and too perishable to take on the long journey.

Elizabeth Dixon Smith "laid in our flour, cheese and crackers, and a large vial of peppermint essence"; and Keturah Belknap, before she left Iowa, made "a lot of crackers and fry doughnuts, cook a chicken, boil ham, and stew some dryed fruit." Belknap thought that these foods would last a week and would give the company time to get used to campfire cooking. David De Wolf wrote his wife that they had "first rate hams, codfish, herring, flour, hard bread, . . . chocolate, rice."[87]

The cheese the emigrants carried was probably a type of Cheddar since that was the variety usually sold in grocery stores in the 1850s. In New England, Cheddar was often referred to as "store cheese or American cheese." In 1845 grocery stores in St. Joseph, Missouri, described their cheese as "common" or West-reserve cheese. Com-

44

mon cheese was the cheapest. Albert Bolles has written that most of the cheese being processed was of the skimmed-milk variety: "little attempt has been made in this country to manufacture the more delicate and richer cheeses for which the Old World is so famous; instead, there is a great temptation to rob the cheese of part of its richness for butter."[88]

Until about 1830 cheese was made in this country almost exclusively by farmers, who then exchanged it for groceries and dry goods. Only small quantities were made, and no one seemed concerned about trading in larger amounts. Finally, an astute farmer in Herkimer, New York, realized that with a more systematic production process in the cheese industry, he would make larger profits. As the countryside became dotted with dairy houses, cheese production in Herkimer County received a reputation for excellence. By 1866, the last years of the great expeditions to the West, there were 500 cheese factories in New York.

When cheese was made at home, the kind might vary from a simple soft cheese to an aged European-type cheese such as Cheshire or Stilton. Early recipe books list both kinds. Soft cheese was made by dripping heated milk through a filter and pressing the curds in a mold. The rennet, used in cheesemaking to separate the curds (the solid portion) from the whey (the liquid), came from the stomach of cows. An early cookbook writer reported that "there is great difference in the strength of rennets; some will make a thousand weight of cheese, while others will scarcely make fifty. Experience alone will teach exactly how much to use."[89] The soft cheeses had to be eaten within a few days; otherwise, they would spoil. Soft cheese may have been the type that Helen Carpenter's California-bound wagon train unfortunately bought at Fort

Kearny. Carpenter complained that it "should have been 'mustered' out long ago, it is too old to be in service. One mere taste took the skin off the end of my tongue."[90]

Cheese spoiled or left a bad taste because it was made from nonrefrigerated milk that had soured or because the milk had come from cows whose diet included bitter weeds or plants such as onions, turnips, and garlic. Many words were written about the care and feeding of milk cows; one writer went so far as to suggest withholding water if the cow did not drink the skimmed milk that was "good for her." Carrots were considered a good vegetable for cows. And of course special directions were given for keeping all utensils used in cheesemaking scrupulously clean.

Naturally not everyone followed the suggestions offered or added extras to their basic list of provisions. Traveling across the continent was expensive, and price was important; so was the availability of goods and space in the wagon. Not every food, regardless of the demand, could be purchased or carried. Hence the decisions for stocking the wagon wheel kitchen were an important first step in preparing for travel along the Oregon-California Trail.

But there were many meals to cook, and surely the thought of a new food item or a better grind of flour was enticing. The large number of emigrants inspired the nation's farmers, merchants, and manufacturers to provide food that was not only appealing to the palate but also stable enough to last through the long westward journey. "[The proprietor] hopes that by keeping a well selected stock, and selling at the lowest market rates, he will merit and receive a share of public patronage," stated one merchant in the *St. Joseph Gazette*, April 28, 1852. Judging from the many advertisements in newspapers and magazines, we can believe that many people apparently shared that sentiment.

2

THE MOBILE PANTRY

In order to make the journey to the West with their belongings, most of the emigrants, especially those with families, built or bought a covered wagon. Nicknamed the prairie schooner, this early mobile home was basically a long farm wagon with a high canvas covering. Constructed so that it was strong enough to carry 2,000 to 2,500 pounds of goods and yet light enough so that the animals pulling the wagon were not overburdened, the prairie schooner was living room, kitchen, bedroom, and storage room for four to six months. Making it comfortable enough for people to sit and sleep in was a prime consideration.

A good-sized wagon allowed women and children to accompany their husbands and fathers and also held large amounts of equipment so that people could travel with some of the comforts of home. And the storage space of the mobile pantry altered the cooking scene: For the first time, travelers carried stoves or packed favorite kitchen implements to make food preparation easier. They could cushion fresh eggs in a bag of grain or tuck in a jar of preserves to be used on a special occasion. Moving long distances by covered wagon might not have been luxurious but it was better than traveling with only pack-mules.

"Pilgrims on the Plains." Sketch from *Harper's Weekly* (1869).
Courtesy of the Kansas State Historical Society, Topeka,
Kansas.

Twenty to twenty-five wagons with about four people
to a wagon were considered a good number for a wagon
train. Unless a large party from one city decided to travel
together, the usual arrangement was to find like-minded
companions in the jumping-off-towns. The lure of the West
appealed to a wide variety of folks so that one found the
rich and the poor, the educated and the illiterate, the religious and the nonbelievers traveling together. Abigail
Scott described her company:

We have a fair specimen here tonight of the various
occupations of different persons in the (*world*): Bet-
ting and playing cards is going on at one encamp-

ment, music and dancing at another, while at a third persons are engaged singing religious hymns and psalms with apparent devotion.[1]

Traveling in a self-contained wagon that carried all the cooking supplies and implements had certain advantages. When the group decided to stop for meals, instead of spending time looking for food the travelers focused their attention on preparing the meal and on finding a suitable campsite near fresh water, fuel, and grass. Those tasks were not so easy. Picking a campsite that had water, fuel, and grass was a formidable challenge for people following guidebooks that were not always up-to-date or even accurate. For example, if the guide had been written in a year when numerous storms had filled the rivers, then plenty of water could be found. But in another year the travelers might find streams dried up and the expected water gone. And during the years of heavy travel, a wagon train might arrive at a campsite that was already filled or that had been stripped of grass by earlier travelers. In such cases, tired or not, the exhausted drivers had to continue.

Simply making a cup of hot coffee at the end of the day required that someone fill a container with clean water, gather some fuel, start a fire, and grind and roast the coffee beans. An hour or more might pass before the aroma of freshly brewed coffee drifted over the parking space. And such a coffee break occurred only when it did not rain. On rainy days, every bit of ingenuity was called into action as the travelers figured out ways to keep the fire going. An English emigrant offered one solution for the problem of cooking in the rain:

Another difficulty was how to find firewood with which to cook supper. An armful being gathered, I had to sit over it to keep it dry while lighting it—like a rooster hovering something that needed protection—the rain still falling steadily. At length—three quarters of an hour—the fire was kindled. Then the smoke made my eyes smart so I had to give way, which liked to prove fatal. But putting on the frying pan bottom up, I had an iron umbrella, and a fire in spite of the rain. The difficulty of cooking supper overcome, we had the pleasurable exercise of eating it—no small luxury, for our breakfast had consisted of raw ham, pilot bread and cold water.[2]

Most emigrants were not so determined. After an exhausting day of travel, if heavy rains came, preparing a supper of cold hardtack was easier than fighting the elements.

MAKING THE WAGON

Making or purchasing a well-constructed wagon was essential if the pioneers' self-contained mobile pantries were to survive the trip west and offer some semblance of a home-away-from-home. Of prime importance was the choice of wood for the wagon's base. Guidebook writers and emigrants who had made the trip seemed to agree that the wagon must be made from good, seasoned hardwood: hickory for the bows supporting the canvas-covering and oak or maple for the wagon bed. S. H. Taylor wrote that when the wagons were passing over the plains, if the timber was not well seasoned, "every seam in woodwork opens."[3] Nathan Putnam advised that if the wagon were to withstand the dry climate of the plains and the numerous river crossings, the base had to be constructed from the "best kind [of wood] and *well Seasoned.*"[4] And Peter Burnett warned, "When you reach the mountains, if your wagons are not well made of seasoned timber, the tires become loose."[5] No wonder the story of seasoning the wood became a favorite of Betsey Bayley's family; her granddaughter reported that "[Daniel Bayley] had seasoned this wood two years, boiled in oil, chosen every piece himself, and like the great Temple of Solomon there was no unworthy piece found therin. Strong and tough but light."[6]

Emigrants did not always build their own wagons. Many parties waited until they arrived in the jumping-off-towns and then purchased their vehicles from a commercial establishment. St. Louis, Independence, and St. Joseph had resident wagon builders. David Stearns, a carpenter in Independence, "had the running gears of four or five wagons built in a nearby shop, while he built the wagon boxes and fitted them with hoops and oiled canvass covers, made a supply of ox yokes and bows for the outfit."[7]

The men and women who depended on others to build the vehicles could only hope that those carpenters who made and supplied wagons adhered to the recommendation to use seasoned wood. Purchasing a poorly constructed wagon resulted in serious difficulties. J. A. Forrest's advertisement in the *St. Joseph Gazette*, April 28, 1852, suggests that his wagons were built according to the best specifications.

Oregon & California

The subscriber would inform every person in this and the adjoining counties, and especially the Oregon and California emigrants, that he has on hand a very large lot of wagons suitable for the Oregon and California expedition. The undersigned has been to California, and feels confident he knows the wants of emigrants much better than those who have not been to that country. He will further say, that he can and will sell upon as good terms as any other house west of St. Louis. Having a Wagon shop attached to the Blacksmith shop, he is prepared to do all kinds of work in wood and iron and at the shortest notice, and in the best of style.

There were two parts to the covered wagon; the wagon bed or box and the undercarriage or running gear. The bed or box was the floor of the living quarters and held the provisions. The running gear controlled the wheels and steering mechanism and was the most crucial part of the vehicle.[8]

The construction of the wagon bed was really quite simple. The carpenter made a box nine to ten feet long and about four feet wide with sides two feet high that were either straight or flared. The size varied according to the emigrant's needs but it had to be light enough not to overburden the animals pulling it. Chester Ingersoll suggested that home-built wagons eleven feet long and built on the wide track were superior. The ones he found in Independence were "poorly ironed, heavy wooded, and cost from $90 to $100 each."[9]

Flared sides, according to Peter Burnett, were best because the water would run down the outside of the wagon. The parts were mortised together, and if done properly no nails were used. Family members added special touches to fit their needs and took pride in their homes. "I thought it the best looking wagon in the crowd, our bows sat so nice and round," wrote Susan Walton, describing her family's wagon.[10]

Most wagons were single-decked, but diarists tell about adding a floor or a platform to create a two-storey vehicle. In one compartment the family stored the provisions; the other was used for living quarters. Turning living quarters into a bed was a daily event, and travelers devised various schemes. In one of the Scott family's wagons "a feather bed and pillows, rolled together and tied with cord during the day, were at night made up for a couch, with quilts and blankets, in a space made vacant by the removal of the boxes."[11] A similar arrangement was carried out by a couple traveling with Harriet Buckingham. "Mr. & Mrs. Smith have had the carriage so arranged that a bed can be made of the seats, & when the curtains are all buttoned down there is a comfitable sleeping apartment." In contrast, Charlotte Stearns Pengra complained that her bed was "a thin cotton matrass laid on not the most evenly laid boards, in a space three feet wide for three of us, not room enough for one of us."[12] She does not mention where the mattress was stored during the day. Elisha Perkins divulged that one of the emigrants in his mess "laid across a couple of chests . . . but the sharp edges cut considerably into his arrangements & he was exclaiming against camp life half the night."[13]

Some of the accessories to the wagons that the emigrants added seem quite practical. Stephen Taylor made his wagon more homelike by removing the rockers from a Boston rocker and attaching the chair to the wagon bed; thus his wife Abigail had a place to sit while driving the team.[14] The Ivins party added long boxes along the side that Virginia Wilcox Ivins found useful for storing "sewing materials and other odds and ends dear to the housewife's heart." The Ivins had constructed the backboard of the wagon so that it was "let down with chains so as to form a cupboard wherin were stored provisions for daily use and was most convenient for preparing meals."[15] The Burts, who were traveling with ten children, surrounded the wagon

> with seats that projected out over the wheels. Here the young people of the family, seven girls and three boys sat when the roads were good, spending their time in spelling, reciting history, singing, geography and the multiplication tables and other, and much better songs. It was called "the Band Wagon."[16]

THE PROVISIONS BOX

The all-purpose provision boxes came in all styles and shapes, from a basket to a trunk, and occupied the place of honor in the mobile pantry. These large containers held the food and cooking implements the emigrants would need for the trek west. The boxes had to be placed securely and conveniently in the wagon; they had to fit tightly to keep from rattling and from spilling the contents when the wagons bounced over dirt roads and made the awkward climb over mountains. Yet every day the boxes had to be unpacked before meals could be prepared and thus needed to be easily accessible to the cook. Helen Carpenter described that daily task;

> From the time we get up in the morning until we are on the road it is hurry-scurry to get breakfast and put away the things that necessarily had to be pulled out last night. While under way there is no room in the wagon for a visitor. Nooning is barely long enough to eat a cold bite and at night all the cooking utensils and provisions are to be gotten about the camp fire

Interior of an emigrant wagon. Courtesy of the Jefferson National Expansion Memorial, National Park Service.

and cooking enough done to last until the next night. Although there is not much to cook, the difficulty and inconvenience in doing it amounts to a great deal.[17]

Pioneers put together creative designs for packing the provisions. Keturah Belknap meticulously planned each detail of overland traveling and noted in her journal how she used every bit of wagon space:

Our wagon is backed up to the steps; we will load at the hind end and shove the things in front. The first thing is a big box that will just fit in the wagon bed. That will have the bacon, salt and various other things; then it will be covered with a cover made of light boards nailed on two pieces of inch plank about 3 inches wide. This will serve us for a table. . . . Now we will put in the old chest that is packed with our clothes and things we will want to wear and use on our way. The till is the medicine chest; then there will be cleats fastened to the bottom of the wagon bed to keep things from slipping out of place. . . . The next thing is a box as high as the chest that is packed with a few dishes and things we wont need till we get thru. And now we will put in the long sacks of flour and other things. . . . There is a corner left for the wash-tub and the lunch basket will just fit in the tub. The dishes we want to use will all be in the basket. . . . Now we will fill the other corner with pick-ups. The iron-ware that I will want to use every day will go in a box on the hind end of the wagon like a feed box.[18]

The Judson family solved the problem of placing the provisions by ordering a wagon made with a one-foot projection on each side, "which enabled us to cord up our bed in the back end and to stow away our provisions under it, leaving room in front for our cooking utensils, where they would be convenient to lift out and into the wagon."[19] Other emigrants constructed their own built-in cupboards for storing food and cooking equipment and assembled special platforms for holding stoves. Unfortunately, despite the best packing, the wind was strong enough to "blow our buckets and pans from under the wagons, and this morning we found them (and other things which were not secured) scattered all over the valley," reported Amelia Knight.[20]

In order to save space and cut down on weight, the overlanders packed items designed to do double duty. The provision box could function as a table or a bed, the milk can as a churn. The Belknap family went to some trouble to construct a table from their provision box. They drilled holes in the corners of the box and at mealtime slipped in sticks that served as table legs. Improvising further, Keturah Belknap attached a stick handle to her workbasket, providing her son with a toy covered wagon so that he could play "going to Oregon." Belknap was determined that her family be comfortable. Innovation played a key role in getting the overlanders to their new homes.

SPARKLING WHITE TOPS

After ascertaining that seasoned wood was available and building the box, the wagonmaker had to construct the upper body. The box without its familiar white top was just a wagon; with its covering, the traveling wagon became a home, offering protection from dust, sun, wind, and rain. Making a proper cover was just as important as making a proper base.

The usual method for building a frame was to form a hoop with hickory bows, attach these to the wagon base, and enclose the wooden frame under a cover. A five-foot hoop was considered adequate for providing enough head room so that a person could stand up in the center. Helen Carpenter's family made their hoop square to provide extra headroom, but she doesn't say if this arrangement resulted in rainwater collecting on top.

Heavy, rainproof canvas, well-oiled linen, white muslin, sailcloth, or oil cloth made the best rainproof covering. The overlanders either purchased the covers or made them at home before starting the trip. Keturah Belknap sewed their muslin cover "by the light of a dip candle"; she made it double thick "so we can keep warm and dry." She put the muslin on first and then covered that with heavy linen. "They both have to be sewed real good and strong and I have to spin the thread and sew all these long seams with my fingers."[21] Along with sewing these covers and the clothes for family members, the hardworking women stitched pockets in the canvas covering to hold combs and mirrors or a favorite small cooking implement.

Other travelers offered suggestions for making a waterproof covering. Abigail Scott wrote to her grandfather that the women in her wagon made their cover double thick because "one thickness of Osnaburgs cotten is not sufficient to keep off heavy rains." Peter Decker's company must have agreed with that complaint because they applied "one coat of linseed oil and bees wax mixed by boiling" to their Osnaburg cover, which changed from white to sand color.[22] Mary Hite Sanford's group used three widths of material to cover the bows and two additional widths to form a double cover that would shed rain. Sanford's mother also made their tent, which "was about 9 ft. X 11 ft., all sewed by hand. There were many buttonholes to be worked."[23] She had help from the other women in her town. As they sat diligently sewing up covers and tents, did they envy Sanford's mother or were they glad it was she, not they, going on such a trip?

Chester Ingersoll who departed from Independence, Missouri, in 1847 advised the traveler to leave the covering off "until he arrives at his point of destination or rendezvous, as he can get it done here better for the trip and as cheap as at home—many are not suitable for the journey, besides they get badly torn on the Missouri Bottoms."[24] And Decker reported, "Wagon covers are frequently taken off in traveling on account of the almost constant high wind which sweeps over the prairie like over the ocean meeting with no obstructions by nature or art."[25] Unfortunately, none of the canvas covers was completely waterproof, and the emigrants and their belongings often got wet when the wind blew the rain through the tents and wagon covers. that is, unless the wagons were covered with India rubber.

Besides leaking, the white cover had another drawback: It reflected heat. On sunny days, the bright sunshine bouncing off the dazzling white covers blinded those travelers walking or riding nearby. To help make the wagon cooler and to reduce the glare, emigrant women lined the white covers with colored muslin. Another group, on a particularly hot day in California, moved their wagons close together and "spread an orning which we made of our Tents."[26] To ward off the bright light as they walked by the wagons, men and women wore wide-brimmed head coverings. Too much sun was just one of the many hazards that went with overland travel.

Once the cover was draped over the bows, it had to be secure enough that the winds would not blow it off, yet open enough to provide access and ventilation. To accomplish this requirement, the canvas covering was drawn together by a strong cord at one end to form a tight circle and then, according to Kate Scott, was fastened to the front bow and closed by means of "a canvas door, thrown backward over the wagon sheet when opened, and fastened with large horn buttons when closed."[27]

PROTECTING THE PROVISIONS

Keeping the interior of a wagon dry was a primary concern of the wagonbuilders; threatening winds and fierce rains could play havoc with a wagon's waterproof covering and wooden sidings. Heavy wheels that had to support 2,000 pounds of goods and people could break down or become mired in mud. Taking the wagons across rivers often meant that many of the goods turned into a soggy mess or ended up in the water instead of in the all-purpose provision box. In minutes, storms turned the camping grounds into islands surrounded with muddy water, and soaked the food supplies. The dread of rain was constant as the emigrants fretted about sleeping in wet clothes in wet beds or worried about making bread when the dough was so wet "it almost turned to *batter*."[28]

Rain was not the only cause of wet clothes and soggy food. Water often seeped through the wagon's boards during river crossings. Emigrants experimented with several methods to make their wagons somewhat waterproof. If the river was not too deep they raised the wagon bed by setting it on bolsters. This method was called "blocking" and elevated the bed about two and a half feet. If water reached the blocked-up boxes, extra caulk was applied to all joints and cracks. Large wagon wheels also helped but only on firm river beds. When the ground was soaked the heavy wheels sank, and the wagon had to be pulled out. Stout rope for pulling the wagon out of the mud and caulking material for closing cracks were classified as standard equipment on the wagons. They dangled outside the prairie schooner, along with the milk and water cans.

Finally, if the overlanders determined that the water would come over the bolsters and the wheels, they built a raft and ferried themselves across. At many river crossings commercial enterprises were set up and emigrants could hire someone else to do the job. It was not uncommon for campsites to develop on both sides of the river as wagons lined up and waited their turn to cross. But none of the methods was completely foolproof; many times after a storm a river was unusually menacing and nothing worked. Everything got wet. "I suppose the affair was a trifle for this journey," a sad Lucy Cooke wrote to her relatives after discovering her provision box filled with water.

> I cried with vexation but finding it did no good set to work & took everything out & hung up to dry my towels & tablecloths were all wringing wet & so stained also Sissy's white clothes which I had so nicely starched & ironed ready for her use on arriving at Sacramento.[29]

To keep themselves and their possessions dry, emigrants were advised to pack their belongings in oilcloth and India-rubber carpet sacks. "A few pieces of clothing and our oil cloth suits proved to be all that could be included in this list," noted George McCowen, after the group decided to strip down to necessities.[30]

Goods made of or covered with India rubber were most likely to stay dry. Made from the juice or milk of East Indian rubber tree, *ficus elastica*, India rubber was the Gore-

Tex of the mid-nineteenth century. The product first had been used for making erasers and overshoes, and these articles had appeared in the United States in the early 1800s. Nevertheless, not until Charles Goodyear figured out how to make rubber retain its elasticity at all temperatures did manufacturers realize that India rubber could be used to make ordinary goods waterproof.

To accomplish this process the garmentmakers took the vulcanized rubber and by using pressurized rollers, forced the rubber into and through the cloth. The cloth was then cut out; the edges were covered with rubber cement, folded together, and rubbed down to make a seam. Next, the garment was cured with powdered sulphur, boiled in potash lye, and washed. At this stage it was ready for sale. "The goods made by this machinery are elegant, and the operation of making them is very simple and yet complete.—The invention is Yankee, and no nation can approach us in this kind of work yet," reported the *Scientific American* in 1848.

Goodyear's process was so successful that by 1839, just a few years before the wagon trains began rolling westward, India-rubber clothing, boots, shoes, and implements of all descriptions were readily available for purchase. The producers had found a market where thousands of people needed clothing and provision bags that would stay dry. An advertisement from the *St. Joseph Gazette*, April 12, 1850, reflected India rubber's diversity: "coats, leggins, capes, water tanks, water buckets, tumblers, bottles, cloths of all widths." Even an India-rubber mattress turned up in the Frink family's wagon. The air mattress was inflated at night, and during the day the family let the air out in order to have more room. The Frinks also carried the more traditional feather bed and feather pillows.

Testimonies from a few satisfied customers under-score the success of India-rubber goods. When Elisha Perkins discovered that his India rubber cap and leggings had been picked up by a passing wagon train, he was so upset that he saddled a pony and rode six miles to get them back. "Without them I should have been in an un-comfortable predicament exposed to every storm with no protection," explained Perkins, relieved to have found them.[31] James Hutchings acknowledged that his India-rubber coat "kept me quite dry above but—my pantaloons and socks!"[32] One wonders why Hutchings did not get a longer coat or rubber leggings and boots. But the best en-dorsement for India-rubber goods comes from Solomon Carvalho, who was traveling with packmules instead of a covered wagon.

> They were the most useful articles we had with us; we placed the India-rubber side on the snow, our buffalo robes on top of that for a bed, and covered with our blankets, with an India-rubber blanket over the whole—India-rubber side up, to turn the rain. . . . During the whole journey, exposed to the most furi-ous snow-storms I never slept cold, although when I have been called for guard I often found some diffi-culty in rising from the weight of snow resting on me.[33]

LIGHTENING THE LOAD

Those people going to Oregon Territory knew that they would find few stores selling furnishings and supplies for the home. And since the overlanders also wanted to be comfortable while traveling, they took special pains to

Interior of a covered wagon. Courtesy of the National Archives, Washington, D.C. (#69-N-19519).

make their wagons livable. "Through all the winter preceding the April morning when the final start was made, the fingers of the women and girls were busy providing additional stores of bedding and blankets," recalled Kate Scott.[34] Despite the warnings to leave large or heavy items at home, "the emigrants have waggons fitted up in the best possible style, carpeted, with chairs, bed and looking glass for the convenience of families," reported a writer to the *Missouri Republican*.[35] Nathan Putnam advised his parents that when they made the trip, for sheer comfort, "You should have a *Privy* arraigned in one of the wagons made in the hind part of the wagon." Perhaps because his own rig did not have one, he felt it imperative to recommend such a practical addition; ordinarily, basic hygiene was not a subject for discussion in letters and journals.

Unfortunately, most of the prized possessions of the overlanders ended up decorating the road. Bacon, beans, and abandoned furniture were left all along the trail. Even before he left Independence, Putnam wrote to his father that "we had dispenced with our large Boxes and all our Barrels as they were too heavy to carry." Abigail Scott confessed to her grandfather that "we have thrown away almost every trunk we started with and oil-cloth and India rubber carpet sacks in their stead."[36]

Eventually the emigrants realized that lightweight wagons traveled best. When Lodisa Frizzell's family left their trunks, chests, barrels, and boxes behind, they estimated that the removal "relieved the waggon, of at least 300 lbs."[37] Emigrants soon discovered that they could reduce the weight of the provision boxes by switching to lightweight containers. "All of your flour, bread, rice, sugar, &c., must be put in sacks, as nothing can be carried in barrels," advised Chester Ingersoll. He believed that "the emigrant had better prepare his own [sacks] at home of the best materials, to hold about two or two and a half bushels, as they will pack the best."[38] Keturah Belknap followed his advice and made her own linen bags: four large sacks that would each hold 125 pounds of flour, one for 125 pounds of cornmeal, and a number of smaller ones for dried apples, beans, rice, and coffee.[39]

Responding to the emigrants' problems, one mill in 1850 made a special point of advertising in the *St. Louis Missouri Republican* that their flour was packed in bags:

California Flour O'Fallon Mills
We are prepared to contract for from five to fifteen
hundred, fifty lb packages of flour in double sacks.
The first sack to be of good cotton sheeting and the
outside sack to be of smoke tanned buffalo or elk
skins or what is commonly known as Indian
lodgeskins. Our experience in regard to those packages of smoked and leather sacks, warrants us in rec-
ommending them not only as convenient and safe
packages but . . . they are the best keeper of flour that
has ever been tried in crossing the plains or in camp.
We sold about 1,000 last spring and have abundant
testimony that their being the best that went to California.[40]

If the emigrants did not begin discarding goods
shortly after their departures they usually did so by the
time they reached Fort Laramie, where they had to prepare for crossing the Rocky Mountains. Worn-out animals
and tired people needed all the relief they could get; a
lighter load was a big help. By that point of the trip all the
travelers knew the hazards of carrying too much weight.
They had learned that a frying pan worked as well over a
makeshift oven as in a stove, that a much-loved decorative
bowl with no function was useless, and even that extra
flour was too heavy. Forty-niners often dubbed Fort Laramie as "Camp Sacrifice" because of the massive unload-
ing that took place there by the many wagon trains.
Elisha Perkins wrote that near Fort Laramie one train reported throwing away a "ton of bacon, several barrels of
bread, six dozen steel shovels, axes hose &c &c, amount-
ing in value to nearly 1,500 dollars!" Perkins, to his delight, was able to acquire "about 90 lbs of the finest crackers I have see & are far superior to our own." Perkins's

crackers had been "ground to a fine powder" after his party had packed them in sacks instead of in boxes.[41]

In the final push over the mountains, even a rolling pin was deemed to be too heavy. After two months of traveling, the capable Helen Carpenter had to throw hers away. Mrs. Matthew Deady, who journeyed to Oregon Territory in 1846, captured the agony of discarding favorite possessions:

> A man named Smith had a wooden rolling pin that it was decided was useless and must be abandoned. I shall never forget how that big man stood there with tears streaming down his face as he said, "Do I have to throw this away? It was my mothers. I remember she always used it to roll out her biscuits and they were awful good biscuits."[42]

Although discarding the heavier baggage reduced the weight, it did not solve other problems. Peter Decker complained that when "we changed boxes for sacks it is difficult to make the bed level."[43] Elisha Perkins was concerned that the crackers packed in sacks "will probably be ground to fine powder," which did happen; several weeks later he wrote, "Our crackers were all jammed into 'spoon victuals' already by the shaking they have undergone thus far." Perkins, in spite of his complaining, took the philosophical approach, however. "This tho will be quite a saving to our teeth for they are as hard as the 'nether mil stone.' "[44] Making light of problems went along with lightening the load.

THE BUCKET OF TAR

The bucket of tar dangling from every wagon that rumbled to the West was honored in the official song of the Oregon Pioneer Association at its forty-third reunion:

Tar bucket (ca. 1850). Courtesy of Walt and Jackie Williams (photographer, Howard Giske).

> Wait for the wagon,
> The linchpin wagon,
> The linchpin wagon
> With its bucket of tar.[45]

For the pioneers the tar bucket symbolized the mishaps and marvels of crossing half the country, reminding them that traveling by covered wagon to the Pacific Coast was not for the fainthearted.

The grease or tar bucket that swung from the rear axle was essential. Usually made from a hollowed-out log and fitted with a cover that had a hole for inserting a dip stick these buckets are now considered collectors' items. My husband and I bought one made from a single piece of wood that is well carved and decorated and that now has a lovely patina; the blackened interior still gives off a faint smell of oil. Our bucket, like many others, once held the lubricant to grease the wheels and the other moving parts of the wagon. As Susan Walton recalled, the linchpin wagon "would holler for tar from that old bucket hanging in the rear."[46]

The lubricant was tar or resin mixed in equal parts with tallow, but emigrants used lard or other cooking grease if real tar was unavailable. Sometimes even buffalo or wolf grease ended up in the tar bucket. When some overlanders found an oil seep, they used the oil as a lubricant. In addition to its use as tar and shortening, lard was administered to animals as a remedy for drinking too much alkaline water. John Steele said the lard worked if it was melted and poured into the animal's stomach immediately after it drank the poisoned water, but "after a little delay there seemed to be no remedy."[47]

SIGNS OF THE TIMES

To add a bit of color and fun, wagons displayed signs that identified the company, announced the destination, or made a political statement. Some of the names recounted in the diaries included Pioneer Line; Prairie Bird; Tempest; Albatross; Old Settlers of Keoduk, Pike County, Mo, for California or Bust; T. F. Royal for Oregon; Oregon 54 40—all or none!; and Have you Saw the Elephant?

The sign Oregon 54 40—all or none! surely elicited the most comment and set off political haggling. The slogan, originating in the western states, was coined during the debate over the annexation of Oregon and the extension of the international boundary to 54°40' north latitude. President John Tyler in 1844 made the demand to extend the boundary a formal proposal, but Lord Aberdeen, the British negotiator, stood firm for holding the boundary at 49 degrees. James Polk reiterated Tyler's request when he became president in 1845, but since the United States was soon to go to war with Mexico over the occupation of California, Polk prudently decided against fighting the British. Lord Aberdeen took advantage of the situation and again proposed the 49-degree latitude; Polk accepted and the Senate consented.[48]

OXEN OR MULES?

Most companies chose oxen to pull the wagons, but almost everyone who decided to go west endlessly debated the various advantages of using, oxen, mules, or even horses. Each animal had its supporters. Horses traveled faster but were not as strong, and they suffered hoof damage on the rocky roads and required special feed. Mules and oxen would eat almost any grass and could carry larger loads, but they were slow and stubborn. Oxen constantly won the vote; they were cheaper than mules, were thought to have more endurance on a long trip, and were believed to be less likely to stampede. A four-to-six-yoke team was needed for each wagon. If at least six oxen were attached with a yoke to the wagons, the animals could walk rather than pull and consequently did not wear themselves out so quickly. Yokes, made from wood, were about four feet long, six inches wide, and were made with an up-and-over curve at each end. Emigrants were advised to make the yokes strong but light.

In 1849 there were so many oxen for sale in Independence, Missouri, that James Pritchard wrote, "Such were the crowded condition of the Streets of Ind by long traines of Ox teams mule teams men there with stock for Sale and men there to purchase stock that it was all most impossible to pass along."[49] Oxen sold for fifty to sixty-five dollars per head that year.

ADDING FOOD TO THE PANTRY

Although excess food and heavy equipment had to be dumped to lighten the load as the emigrants reached Fort Laramie, staple foods and extras such as fresh vegetables were purchased along the way. When the supply of staples was low (a problem during the last months of travel) or fresh food was available, the overlanders bought or bartered at the established forts or at the trading posts that began popping up along the trail. Run by former mountain men and Native American entrepreneurs who were more than happy to sell goods and advice to the weary emigrants, these small business establishments were crude, temporary structures set up to meet the emigrants' need for provisions. "We purchased Indian corn, peas, and Irish potatoes [from friendly Indian traders]. . . . I have never tasted a greater luxury than the potatoes we ate on this occasion. We had been so long without fresh vegetables," wrote Peter Burnett near the end of his travels to the Northwest.[50] And in 1853 the twin sisters Cecelia Adams and Parthenia Blank were happy to stop and pay "a man that had groceries and potatoes to sell at 1½ cts per pound."[51] Those fresh vegetables were the first they had seen since leaving home.

Prices and supplies fluctuated widely during the migration to the West Coast. Small business establishments had no control over the food source; they had to rely on the supplies the packers brought in, goods that previous overlanders had traded, and game caught for fresh meat. Additional forces outside their control had a major impact on prices. A good harvest and few overlanders would cause prices to drop, but bad weather and large numbers of people raised the price of goods. Add to that the fact that emigrants never knew when they might need extra food, and it is clear that finding the right supplies for the right prices was clearly a hit-or-miss situation.

For the emigrants who had spent most of their money outfitting the wagons and paying fees at river crossings, prices charged for goods usually seemed high. But the variation in prices for one year can be illustrated by the Sutton family's experience. The Suttons emigrated in 1854, a year when only 10,000 others traveled west. At the first establishment, "7 or 8 log huts and a bakery and store," flour was twenty dollars per 100-weight sack and bread twenty-nine cents per pound. "Mr. Sutton said before he would give that he would live on dumplins." A month later the Suttons met two or three traders, who told them that flour, when available, sold for "26 dollars per 100. whiskey was 2 dollar and A half A pint, cheese 50 cents A pound." Again, the Suttons did not make any purchases. Finally, when flour sold for twelve dollars per sack, they added it to their larder. Their train had been traveling for over two months and according to Sutton's estimate had about 500 miles to go. The important fact about the Sutton's experience is that even the best guidebook could not have advised them about the traders' available goods or the prices. Each year brought a different set of circumstances that affected prices; each wagon party had a different set of needs.

Besides buying supplies, the emigrants traded or sold items. The Suttons "bought some salt for 60 cents per pound. sold dried peaches for the same. sold a peck of beans for two dollars."[52] At Wood River in Nebraska, the Burrells sold "the old corn wagon for $5.00 & the lame cow for $7.50." In the Blue Mountains, John Black received a hound from some men at a quartz mill and then traded the hound for fifty pounds of flour "worth here $6.50," which he later sold for $5.00. Helen Carpenter happily purchased a pound of candy for seventy-five cents from a "trader [who] was anxious to get sugar and as we have more than we think will be required for the trip we sold some."[53]

Army outposts such as Fort Kearny, Fort Laramie, and Fort Hall had commercial establishments, as did Salt Lake City. At the army posts the shops run by civilian merchants were called sutler's stores. Here too supplies and prices varied, just as at the smaller posts. In June 1853 James Farmer found "stores here [Fort Laramie] where we can purchase anything we need but very high." Only a month later William Sloan grimly noted "the commissary claimed to be short themselves having had to furnish others who were ahead of us, more than was expected."[54] Amelia Hadley wondered about the stores at Fort Laramie in 1851—"It seems as though I could hardly contrive how they could get goods there"—but she reported that "here [Laramie] you can get almost any thing you want."[55] A year later Mary Bailey wrote that supplies were for sale, but only "if his necessity compells him to give 50 ct a pound for sugar, raisins, $5 for salartus, 50 cts for a paper of tacks."[56] According to Merrill Mattes, "The emigrants who put in an early appearance at the Fort were well taken care of, while late comers took pot luck."[57]

Salt Lake City was off the beaten trail, particularly

for those travelers going to Oregon Territory. If the emigrants chose that route it was to take on additional supplies, trade a worn-out mule for a well-rested horse, secure medical resources, or just see what the Mormons had built. The amount of goods in any year in Salt Lake City would vary, but each year more and more commercial establishments began operating. The emigrants benefited from a plethora of enterprising merchants eager to fill their cash drawers along with the overlanders' provision boxes. In 1850 Lucena Parsons's family feasted on "potatoes & green corn & other vegetables & we think we never saw as good before having so long been without."[58] The Parsons clan, like many emigrants, decided to spend the winter in Salt Lake City. When Mary Bailey's family stopped there in 1852 they picked up "green pease, beans & potatoes. They tasted good. We do not find butter, lard & such things very plenty." Bailey commented that "vegetables plenty although imported & very high. Sugar 40 cts, coffee the same."[59] Mary Burrell spent a day in the city in 1854 and was happy to discover that soda water, ice cream, and cakes were available. Eight years later the Eppersons purchased milk, vegetables, butter, and fresh meat but were annoyed that the Mormons would not sell flour:

> Could get no flour or other necessities, as the sale of such things by Mormons to emigrants was forbidden by the "high and mighty Brigham." They would sell milk, vegetables, butter and fresh meat. An elderly man saw Mr. Epperson when he was refused flour. He came to our wagon after dark, and said that he had plenty of flour, and if Mr. Epperson would go to his house between ten and eleven o'clock, he would let him have what flour he wanted. . . . Mr. Epperson

paid the enormous sum of fourteen dollars per hundred pounds.[60]

Without the availability of goods and services along the trail, many emigrants never would have made it to the West Coast. The amount of supplies recommended in the guidebooks was, as the name implied, just a guide. The overlanders simply lacked the proper information to determine accurately the precise amount of flour or sugar they would need or to imagine how the absence of fresh foods would determine their moods. The emigrants were reluctant to pay extra for these commodities, but one wonders how many people would have finished the journey if enterprising merchants had not carted in bags of flour, pounds of coffee beans, or a can or two of peaches.

Observing that period from the safe distance of one hundred and fifty years, we marvel at the organization and diligence of those people who built and packed the mobile pantry. Packing and unpacking dishes and flour and other supplies day after day demanded both fortitude and an adherence to a tight schedule. "Hurry-scurry days" were the rule—going west was a major undertaking. As the emigrants sewed the bags that would carry the flour, how many of them even imagined the many tasks that would have to be done before they could sit down with a cup of coffee or a piece of bread?

3

ESSENTIAL EQUIPMENT

After packing her Dutch oven, camp kettle, frying pan, tin-plated cups and spoons, bread pan, and rolling pin, Helen Carpenter observed that "what we are to have to eat is going to be of much more importance than how it is cooked or served."[1] Carpenter had her priorities right, but no matter how meager the food supply, it was still necessary to know how to cook on the trail.

Baking bread and pies over an open fire was different from baking in a brick oven or in the new stoves that were just becoming popular. Making coffee from the dirty waters of the Platte River was certainly a contrast to using clear well water. And boiling and baking in heavy cast-iron Dutch ovens and spiders were changes from baking with pottery dishes such as queensware or redware. Moreover, the cook had to think about finding water, obtaining fuel, and building fires. Choosing the best utensils, heat source, and cooking methods would be of key importance to the overlanders in their constant struggle to prepare two to three meals a day.

Selecting the proper utensils was the first step. Which pots could withstand the intense heat from the buffalo-chip campfires and the jarring from the wagon as it rocked and rolled over the rugged plains and prairies? Joel Palmer urged his followers to provide themselves

Cast-iron muffin tin (ca. 1864). Courtesy of the Museum of History and Industry, Seattle, Washington, gift of Mrs. H. A. Foster (photographer, Howard Giske).

with "a dutch oven and skillet of cast metal. . . . Plates, cups, &c., should be of tin ware, as queens-ware is much heavier and liable to break, and consumes much time in packing up. A reflector is sometimes very useful."[2] Lansford Hastings stressed that heavy items should be left behind: "A baking-kettle, frying pan, tea kettle and coffee pot, are all of the furniture of this kind, that is essential."[3] Mary Powers's inventory of "two tin pans, two tea kettles, one dish kettle, one bake kettle, one coffee mill, six knives and forks, six tea spoons, three large table spoons, eight tin and iron cups, one candle stick, eight pounds candles, frying pan, tin and wooden pail, keg for water . . . and accoutrement"[4] shows that emigrants followed the basic advice but added a few nonessentials to make cooking easier. Neither Palmer nor Hastings had

Spider. Courtesy of the Oregon Historical Society Museum Collection.

mentioned a rolling pin or a coffee grinder. Though the extras would eventually have to be discarded to lighten the load, at the outset having these few items from home was important.

Frying pans in those days were sometimes called spiders. The terms spider, frying pan, and skillet were used interchangeably by the overlanders—the name depended on the region of the country they came from. Traditionally a spider was a large frying pan with legs; eighteenth-century spiders also had long handles so that the fire did not scorch the cook. Spiders generally came with lids, which helped the cooking process in two ways: they prevented liquid in the pot from boiling too vigorously, and they were used to hold hot coals. Hot coals on the top and bottom of the pan created the effect of an oven and speeded up cooking. John Zieber in 1853 recorded that "we bought a 'spider' or skillet with a lid."[5] Zieber strongly believed that with a spider and a boiler his party "could dispense with the stove to good advantage."

By the nineteenth century the term spider meant either a frying pan with short legs or a deep cast-iron skillet. The short legs of a cooking vessel acted as a stand and allowed the cook to set the pan directly over the fire or embers. E. S. McComas, who made the journey to Oregon in 1862, praised the versatile frying pan highly. "We will now cook our grub with nothing but a frying pan to cook in but that is enough for two certainly & a frying pan will cook more than we will have to cook in it soon & then we can throw that away."[6] Caroline Clark, who with her family emigrated from England to Utah in 1866, called the pan a skillet and noted that it was useful for a number of cooking tasks: "We bought a skillet to bake our bread in. Sometimes we make pancakes for a change. We also make cakes in the pan, and often bran dumplings with baking powder."[7]

The Dutch oven carried by Helen Carpenter and just about everyone else who made the trip was worthwhile because it served as a built-in bake oven, a soup pot, and an all-purpose pot for stewing and simmering. Frequently referred to as a bake kettle, camp oven, or bake oven, the sturdy, versatile Dutch oven's chief characteristic was the raised edge around the lid, which was meant to hold hot coals while the pan sat in the embers.

Clarence Bagley, a Washington pioneer, described the bake ovens taken along by his group of travelers:

We carried "reflectors" and "bakeovens" to bake our bread in and for other cooking purposes. The latter were big iron pots from twelve to twenty-four inches across the top, which [the lid] was flat with turned-up-edges, thus making a big iron plate. The oven was set on a bed of coals and coals heaped on its top and it did not take long to bake the bread which was wonderfully sweet and palatable.[8]

Cooking pot with legs, "Oregon camp pot" (Dutch oven ca. 1851). Courtesy of the Museum of History and Industry, Seattle, Washington, gift of the estate of Roberta Frye Watt (photographer, Howard Giske).

Commenting on early utensils, culinary historians in 1870 speculated that "when cooking stoves came in, the bake-kettle, or covered skillet, went out, and with it a large part of what was good in our American cookery."[9]

According to one legend, the large, hollow cast-iron pan acquired the name Dutch oven because it was brought to North America by the Pilgrims, who had spent twelve years in Holland before sailing on the *Mayflower*. On that tiny vessel baggage was limited, and there was no room for stoves. To replace the stoves, the Pilgrims carried with them large pots that they used for boiling and baking. To honor the hospitable Dutch, who were good hosts, the early settlers called the pot a Dutch oven.

The reflector oven that Clarence Bagley took with

Tin bird-roaster (tin kitchen, mid-nineteenth century). Courtesy of the Antiques Gallery, Seattle, Washington (photographer, Howard Giske).

him and that Joel Palmer considered practical was also called a tin-kitchen. This handy cooking appliance came into use around 1800 and was available in many shapes and sizes. The most common configuration was a tin cylinder either completely open in the back or with a door that opened. When the pan was in use the open side faced the fire. The combination of direct heat and reflected heat from the rounded side quickly cooked the meat or biscuits. The little door allowed the cook to test the food without moving the oven.[10] A dripping pan for catching the grease, a shelf for baking biscuits and cakes, and either a spit or hooks for roasting meat were optional features. Light-weight, small, and portable, the tin kitchens were ideal for traveling. Emigrants reported that the reflector oven "bakes very nicely."

Resourceful overland cooks such as Catherine Mc-Daniel Furniss constructed a simple reflector oven from a tin can that had part of its side cut out. She placed the dough for rolls in the can and set it near the campfire so that the reflected heat would bake the rolls more quickly.[11] Campers today are still using variations of this cooking device.

UTENSILS MADE OF TIN

The tinware packed in the prairie schooners was made from sheet iron coated with pure tin. The tinning process took place before the sheet steel was made into utensils. Kitchen utensils made of tin have been popular since the seventeenth century, and the first American manufacture of tinware was in Berlin, Connecticut, in 1770.

In the early days tin implements were cast in molds or shaped by the blacksmith, and the parts were soldered to-gether. By the time the emigrants needed quantities of tinware, inventors had discovered a way to stamp out the pieces in one operation. The type of tin coating used deter-mined the quality of the tinware; the better the coating, the better the utensils.[12]

Lightweight, unbreakable, and a good conductor of heat, tinware was the perfect utensil for the trail, that is, if the hot weather did not make the tinware too hot to handle. Then its conductivity became a disadvantage. "The tin pans, plates & handles of the frying pan after setting an hour in the sun, were so hot that actually I

could not hold them without a *holder*," complained
Charles Gray.[13] At least his utensils were intact; Anna
Gatewood, a companion of Ruth Shackleford, "got the
handles melted off all her tin cups."[14] A second disadvantage of the early tinware was that it rusted because min-
ute holes in the tin allowed moisture to reach the iron
base.

Despite its faults, all emigrants used tin. If the overlanders had not brought tin utensils from home, merchants in the
jumping-off-towns were more than happy to sell them some.
Advertisements such as one that often appeared in the *St. Joseph Gazette* in the 1850s let the buyers know that "tin ware,
such as camp kettles, cups, canteens, buckets, boilers, plates"
were available. At a tin shop in Salt Lake City in 1852, Lucy
Cooke purchased a "tin coffee or tea pot" and a "tin bucket
with a lid" for $1.00, a "small bread pan" for $1.50, and a
"small camp kettle (sheet iron with lid)" for $2.00. She felt
the prices were high and complained that they spent "$5½ in
as many minutes."[15]

NEW AND NOTEWORTHY

In his guidebook *Route and Distances to Oregon and California*, J. M. Shively suggests a few different and noteworthy
implements. Written in 1846, the guide was one of the earliest but was not very influential.[16] Still several of the recom-
mendations could be used by today's backpackers as well as
by the overlanders. Shively advised carrying "an iron pan,
the handle so jointed as to fold up; a kind of knife, fork, and
spoon, that all shut in one handle." The combination knife
and fork was available in many hardware catalogs, according to Shively. Linda Franklin, an expert on antique cook-
ware, points out that the one-piece knife and fork was

widely used during the Civil War. A screw running through the center of either the knife or the fork held the cutlery together, and each piece was simply pulled out for use. The patent for the all-in-one knife and fork was just one of many issued in the last half of the nineteenth century. Emigrants going west provided a useful market for trying out new designs. Certainly the all-in-one cutlery tool and the pan with a fold-down handle saved space.

Perhaps emigrants did not listen to Shively's advice because he insulted a large portion of potential travelers:

> However much help your wives and daughters have been to you at home, they can do but little for you here—herding stock, through either dew, dust, or rain, breaking brush, swimming rivers, attacking grizzly bears or savage Indians, is all out of their line of business. All they can do, is to cook for camps.[17]

No doubt many women differed with his pronouncements as they drove the teams, gathered fuel, and ran after stray cows. Susan Angell, Ruth Shackleford, and Harriet Loughary are a few of the early pioneer women whose actions refute Shively's judgment. Angell recorded, "I prepared the meals for our family circle, and took turns in driving the mule team during the day."[18] Loughary complained, "In addition to preparing food and beds for eight in family, I am compelled to harness and drive a four horse team."[19] And Shackleford declared, "Got up by daybreak and went to get wood for the breakfast fire."

USEFUL IMPLEMENTS

Other utensils and practical items that made the list of essentials included butcher knives, coffee mills, water kegs, churns, fishing poles, and rifles. Joel Palmer suggested that "families should each have two churns, one for carrying sweet and one for sour milk."[20] Peter Burnett recommended "a tin canister made like a powder canister" as the best holder for milk.[21] S. H. Taylor advised that "a *can* holding 6 to 20 qts. keeps our sour milk & cream, & makes our butter by the motion of our wagon."[22] Always practical, Burnett recommended a "small grindstone in company, as the tools become dull on the way."[23]

Fishing poles and rifles clearly are not cooking implements, but since the travelers had to procure their own fresh fish, fowl, or meat, the equipment does fit into the category of useful items. Palmer advised each male person to carry "at least one rifle gun, and a shot gun is also very useful for wild fowl and small animals."[24]

Not satisfied with a simple fishing pole, the men in Charles Gray's wagon train used a fishnet, "an invaluable article for us, we imagine, as we can always in pressure supply ourselves with fish in a little while."[25] The fishnet eventually performed well, for several months later Gray boasted that "we went in with our seine & caught about 100 fine fish & made a delicious supper of them. Never do I recollect anything more delightful in the eating line." Unfortunately, George Keller's party did not have a fishnet, but being energetic and enterprising young men they decided to convert their wagon cover into a net. "It was 'no go'; the result of the fishing being a *cold bath*."[26] At least they determined whether the covering was waterproof.

WATER AND VINEGAR

Casks for carrying water came in various sizes and shapes. Joel Palmer recommended bringing one eight- or ten-gallon keg; George Keller's held six gallons, and Margaret Frink had two India rubber bottles that each held five gallons. Frink speculated that these would come in handy during the desert crossing. Finding fresh water was a daily task. If the water keg was empty, dinner was cold hardtack with nothing hot to wash it down.

The rivers defined the route for the overlanders, who mainly followed the Missouri, Platte, and Sweetwater to Fort Hall. At that juncture those people going to California traveled south and then followed the Humboldt River. Those travelers choosing Oregon Territory proceeded along the Snake River and traveled northwest. The route from Fort Kearny (Nebraska) to Fort Laramie (Wyoming) was called the Great Platte River Road.

In certain areas of the country, particularly along portions of the Platte River, finding water safe for drinking and cooking was a problem. Generally it was sullied with noxious bacteria and contained alkalis and other mineral salts. Bernard Reid described certain Platte River valleys as covered with "salt or alkali substance, white as snow and half an inch thick.[27] Many emigrants attributed the recurrent diarrhea to the bad water.

When bad water made them sick some emigrants doctored themselves with vinegar and soon recovered. Popular folklore designated vinegar as an all-purpose drink that cured everything. Vinegar (from the French *vinaigre* or sour wine) is any sour liquid containing from 4 to 12 percent acetic acid. It is made from products such as fruit, grains, beer, cider, and wine that produce alcoholic fermentation. The method for making vinegar was simple and required only the cook's patience to wait for the cider or wine to ferment spontaneously. Because apple cider was such a popular American drink almost every household had a potential supply of homemade vinegar. *The*

Prairie Farmer gave explicit directions for making it (the "bung" is a stopper for the hole through which a cask is filled):

CIDER VINEGAR

Take a clean oaken-barrel, or wine-cask, place it in a warm room; if in the summer time in a hot place where the sun will strike on it; put in one, two, or more gallons of clear fermented cider; leave the bung out, so that the air may have free circulation. In two or three weeks it will be fit for use.[28]

This passive method did not produce the best vinegar, however. If the cook wanted to be sure to make a quality vinegar, a little more effort was required. Eliza Leslie offered such a recipe:

CIDER VINEGAR

Take six quarts of rye meal; stir and mix it well into a barrel of strong hard cider of the best kind; and then add a gallon of whiskey. Cover the cask, (leaving the bung loosely in it,) set it in the part of your yard that is most exposed to the sun and air; and in the course of four weeks (if the weather is warm and dry) you will have good vinegar fit for use. When you draw off a gallon or more, replenish the cask with the same quantity of cider, and add about a pint of whiskey. You may thus have vinegar constantly at hand for common purposes.[29]

Even with everything else they had to do, the emigrants made flavored vinegar from the wild berries growing near the trail. Sophie Goodridge used haw (hawthorn) berries;[30] Eliza McAuley used currants. The practice of making fruit vinegars has been popular for centuries; early cookbooks offer recipes for them. Raspberry vinegar, for example, was considered medicinal. The flavored vinegars were made simply by adding berries and sugar to prepared vinegar, simmering the mixture, and allowing it to sit in the sun for several days. After about a week a piquant vinegar was ready for use.

Vinegar had been used as a medicine for many centuries—Hippocrates prescribed it for his patients. What may have been a new practice was giving a dose of vinegar to sick cows. In his diary E. W. Conyers provides a vinegar remedy for cows that drank too much alkaline water; he credits the recipe to Captain Frémont and testifies that it always worked.

REMEDY FOR COWS

Take one-half pint each of lard and syrup; warm just sufficient to mix good, and if the animal is bloated, add to this one-half pint of good vinegar and drench them immediately.[31]

Abigail Scott made a similar claim: "A dose of vinegar and melasses . . . has the tendency to counteract the effects of the alkali and soda."[32]

CLEARING THE WATER

A common saying among the emigrants was that before they reached Oregon Territory everyone had eaten a "peck of dirt." "I had no idea before what amount of filth a man could eat," J. Robert Brown recorded.[33] To clear their drinking water of much of the river mud and silt, the emigrants used cornmeal as a makeshift filter. A drinking vessel was filled to the top with the muddy water and a handful of cornmeal added. After twenty minutes, the mud, or at least most of it, sank to the bottom with the cornmeal. The water on top would be reasonably clear and was siphoned off with care.[34] If there was not time to wait, the water was drunk, mud and all. "This is what is called seeing one of the Elephants Tracks," Elisha Perkins recorded after a sip of dirty water.[35] When cornmeal was not available, alum (aluminum ammonia sulfate) was substituted. (Alum was also used as an ingredient for making pickles.)

One diarist wrote that the travelers "generally get a pint of mud out of every pail of water,"[36] an enormous amount of dirt, regardless of the size of the pail. Speculating on what would happen if someone "swallows twice his allotted amount of dirt (one peck)," Helen Carpenter took the philosophical approach that their struggles made them "impervious to what would kill ordinary mortals."[37]

Besides clearing dirty water, cornmeal was used to remove the sulphurous taste of the water found in the Humboldt Sink, as James Hutchings reported:

> About one hundred yards from the road . . . we saw several wells, but all the water was salt. One being a little fresher than the rest I took a quart of it, and mixing it with panola [dried, ground cornmeal], drank every drop, and was not thirsty after it, altho the day was hot.[38]

Making instant lemonade was another way of perking up the alkaline water. To create this refreshing drink, the pioneer mixed the water with vinegar or citric acid, sugar, and essence of lemon (lemon extract). Ellen Tootle, however, had to be satisfied with a lemonade substitute, for

"Mr. Tootle brought with him a preparation of lemon (as he thought) but it proved to be tartaric acid and sugar, he had been cheated. It was refreshing, though rather a poor substitute for lemonade."[39] In the nineteenth century, truth in advertising was not uppermost in the minds of the merchants hawking their products. Commercial establishments that advertised in newspapers proclaimed that their goods were the best. The lemon extract promised in the *St. Louis Republican*, March 30, 1850, may have extolled the virtues of the product Mr. Tootle purchased since there was no Food and Drug Administration to protect the consumer. "Concentrated Extract of lemon—This extract is of such strength that a small phial produces more than a gallon of lemonade, thus at all times affording to the emigrant a pleasant beverage. It is highly recommended by physicians as an excellent preventative of scurvy."

When clear, clean water was available everyone rejoiced. "We now can drink this good, cold mountain water to our hearts' content. It seems to give up a new lease of life,"[40] E. W. Conyers recorded; his party had just left the Platte River for the valley of the Sweetwater Mountains. It was a sentiment endorsed by Margaret Frink after drinking "the nauseous stuff of the Humboldt 'sink,' this spring water was more than an ordinary luxury."[41] The Frinks paid packers one dollar a gallon for clear water.

WATER WAS NOT EVERYWHERE

The wagons followed the river routes as best they could, but at times the water disappeared under a sandy bed or changed into a dirty trickle. And at certain places the river followed terrain that would not accommodate the wagons. "Impossible to get water on acount of the banks of the river being so high & difficult to ascend," bemoaned Celinda Hines.

On some days water was not available because it had spilled or because the person responsible for filling the casks forgot or was just too tired to do it. "Owning to our negligence in filling the casks we were without water for dinner," lamented Abigail Scott. That day the Scotts had traveled over twelve hilly miles in "sand six inches deep." Probably she was exhausted rather than negligent. "Camped without water" was a recurring phrase in the emigrants' diaries; they called that situation a "drycamp." Emigrants were advised to keep their water pails full.

At all times water was regarded as a treasured commodity, and keeping the water pails filled was a daily task. Going without water affected the mood of the travelers:

> At a wood, we took in quite a lot & also some water, & before I could get the casks full, the train moved on. Gen. Darcy had no reason for this great hast to get to the diggings! So the consequence was that although we had supper & a little water to wash dishes with—yet we had nothing to drink during the evening when we were thirsty—nothing to wash in the next morning, or cook with till 12'Oclock the next day, when I luckily fill'd 2 canteens with dirty water to drink. This may appear a very small matter, but it was a great annoyance & I merely mention it to show how great a deprivation the loss of a few gallons of water is on the plains.[42]

When there was no river or stream handy, the crafty travelers collected water "from the road," a fine example of making do. They would make a well by digging a hole two to four feet deep in the sandy soil near the river or

"Emigrants Crossing the Plains." Sketch from Samuel Bowles, *Our New West* (1869). Courtesy of the Kansas State Historical Society, Topeka, Kansas.

stream, lower a pail, and haul out water. "Traveled about 19 miles & camped without water or wood. Got some water out of the road. Cold cold cold," complained Mary Burrell.[43] Some overlanders considered this water as superior to that obtained from rivers. Others disagreed and believed that so-called well water was dirty and contaminated with insects. S. H. Taylor took this view and warned that "everyone ought to have too much sense to use water from the stinking holes dug by some foolish persons in the margins of 'slews' and alkaline marshes."[44]

PICK UP A PAIL OF ICE WATER

The Ice Springs in Wyoming were another source of water and a great curiosity to the overlanders. There the emigrants made use of large chunks of ice for cooking by melting them back at the campsite for cooking water. Amelia Hadley described the task: "Here you obtain pure ice by diging down to the depth of 4 to 6 inches. . . . there is a solid cake of ice as clear as any I ever saw and more so cut a piece as large as a pail and took and rapt it in a blanket, to take along camp to night on the river."[45] Hadley does not say whether she liked this water, but Sophia Goodridge definitely did not: It "has a bad smell . . . and not good to use." Bernard Reid warned that it "tastes strongly of alkali."[46]

Undaunted by the bad smell and alkaline taste, the men traveling with James Pritchard added a sprinkling of alcohol to the ice and sat back to enjoy mint juleps. Dr. T——, a companion of Pritchard, recorded the event in his journal: "We gathered several buckets full [of ice], from which we have had Mint Juleps in abundance."[47] Were the doctor and James Pritchard, both Kentuckians, so desirous of carrying on the Bluegrass state's tradition of banishing the cares of the day with a tall, frosty mint julep that they tucked a few sprigs of mint in their provision box? Did they happen to find fresh mint growing nearby? Did they just pretend their cold drink tasted like the one back home? Here is another unsolved culinary mystery, although as one born and raised in Kentucky, I would vote for the third answer, basing my evidence on the fact that "mint juleps in abundance" would make pretending easy.

Actually, Kentuckians were not the only travelers professing a liking for juleps; the drink was popular throughout the country. A julep sipped in the morning was considered a "healthful way to combat fevers, arising from night air and hot climates." The word originally described a nonalcoholic medicinal syrup, but by the mid-eighteenth century, spirits (usually rye or brandy) were being added.

Adding mint is an American innovation; the practice originated in Virginia in the early 1800s, a fact contested by Kentuckians. The mint julep was first made with local whiskey, ordinarily home-distilled, and with homegrown mint. Kentuckians, of course, choose bourbon. The marriage of bourbon and mint forms "a sublime ethereal essence, all divine," noted an early Kentucky poet.[48]

Eleanor Allen employed the same method of obtaining water used by the overlanders at Ice Springs when her group camped near a large snowbank. "I went to it and found it about 3 feet deep, solid snow mixed with ice. When we scraped the top, we cut out lumps of it pure and white. I carried some of it nearly a mile as our train had gone on. . . . But we had a drink of snow water!"[49] "Think of that ye denizens of pent up cities! snow almost in the very heart of summer!" bragged Charles Gray when the men brought a pailful of snow into camp.[50] If they poured molasses or syrup over the snow, the Allen and Gray parties served sugar-on-snow or "jack wax," a half-warm, chewy kind of taffy that was a popular dessert. That would have been something to write home about!

At times the only way to find water was to pick up a pail and go looking. Basil Longsworth recalled, "We had to get our water out of the river and carry it up a hedge of rock sixty or eighty feet high and very steep & then a quarter of a mile to our wagons."[51] "Very laborious," observed Abigail Scott after she had carried water up a one-half-mile-long river bluff.

SPRING WATER—ALL NATURAL INGREDIENTS

The various types of natural spring water that appeared in Wyoming, Idaho, and Utah intrigued everyone, and almost every diarist recorded encountering these phenomena. The Soda Springs, now beneath the waters of the Soda Point Reservoir in Idaho, were especially popular. Parthenia Blank described that natural marvel:

> These consist of springs of water of an alkaline taste bubbling up through the rock and forming mounds of the mineral from 2 to 20 feet high and with bases of proportional size and gas sufficient coming up to keep them constantly boiling like a pot and the opening at the top resembles a large kettle.[52]

The springs were surrounded by a natural stone wall; in some pools the water had a reddish cast. Celinda Hines maintained that it "equalled the best soda water. . . . It boiled up out of the solid rock—as they all do. . . . The vapors has the same effect which the inhaling of hartshorn produces." Hartshorn (smelling salts) is an impure carbonate of ammonia obtained by distilling any kind of bone, particularly that of a hart (the male red deer), hence its name. Enterprising pioneers mixed the spring water with sugar and vinegar, and Abigail Scott claimed it "makes a drink equal to any prepared soda in the States." Despite traveling under less than ideal circumstances or perhaps because of it, the overlanders never lost their taste for variety.

The water at Beer Springs was popular because its taste reminded some emigrants of the taste of small beer, a weak brew that has a long history in this country. Capt. John Frémont speculated that "Beer springs received their name from the voyageurs & trappers . . . who, in the midst of their rude & hard lives, are fond of finding some fancied resemblance to the luxuries they rarely have the fortune to enjoy."[53] That variety of beer first gained notoriety as part of a prison diet of bread and water, or bread and small beer; it was served to prisoners in the days when men were incarcerated in their own houses instead of in prison buildings. By the mid-nineteenth century, when the emigrants were making history, small beer had acquired a new status and was served at social outings, just as we would serve carbonated drinks; it was considered harmless. The recipe from the *New England Economical Housekeeper and Family Receipt Book* demonstrates that it was easy to make.

GOOD, WHOLESOME SMALL BEER

Take two ounces of hops, and boil them, three or four hours, in three or four pailfuls of water; and then scald two quarts of molasses in the liquor, and turn it off into a clean half-barrel, boiling hot; then fill it up with cold water before it is quite full, put in your yeast to work it; the next day you will have *agreeable, wholesome small beer*, that will not fill with wind, as that which is brewed from malt or bran; and it will keep good till it is all drank out.[54]

Eleanor Allen discovered that the water from Beer Springs "[is] the color of beer and taste[s] a little like flat beer."[55] Henry Allyn contrasted the water to the water at Soda Springs:

It boils up from the bottom like a common spring, which keeps the surface in motion, but it is not forced up by gas, like the Sodas, but runs spontaneously. Its taste very much resembles small beer and to me is not at all disagreeable. I drank nearly a pint and it had no bad effect, but set me to belching wind from the stomach, on which it set very light.[56]

97

Other springs that fascinated the emigrants were those in Utah that emitted hot or boiling water; a few unbelievers had burning lips or hands when they tried a cup of it. Jean Baker relates an amusing account of testing the waters:

> I doubted its being so hot as represented, so in order to be convinced, I very cautiously stepped on some pieces of rock, until I stood alone quite close to the bubbling water; by this time I began to believe what I had been told, as my feet began to feel much warmer than pleasant, however determined to make sure, I plunged in my hand, but was glad to draw it out again much to the amusement of my companions.[57]

Always ready to try something new, the emigrants collected the water and used it for cooking. This procedure saved on precious fuel since the water was hot enough to boil an egg or to cook "meat perfectly done in a few minutes."[58] Mary Bailey, an enterprising cook, used the boiling water in a makeshift double boiler. She placed an egg in "fresh water & that in a tin bucket in the hot water" and in a few minutes had a cooked egg.[59] The Bailey contingency had just spent several days in Salt Lake City, where they had purchased "plenty of vegetables to eat & milk & eggs."

"THE CHIPS BURNED WELL"

The emigrants always hoped their campsite would be near a supply of fuel as well as water. Around Fort Kearny, Nebraska, the supply of timber began to diminish and fuel became scarce. Next to "camped without water," "camped without wood" became a repeated complaint.

Even when wood was available, it was often green willow branches. Criticism of green willow from two emigrants testifies to their dislike of it: "It is very trying on the patience to cook and bake on a little green wood fire with the smoke blowing in your eyes so as to blind you, and shivering with cold so as to make the teeth chatter," complained Esther Hanna, a newly married minister's wife.[60] "Cooking has to be done with green willows. This need be tried but once to enable one to give an opinion on this kind of fuel," Helen Carpenter recorded.[61]

The time-consuming and tiring process of cooking over a smoking fire sapped the energy of weary travelers. Harriet Loughary admitted that at times it was easier just to give up:

> After a hard day's work, we of course were hungry but to cook with a fire made of green sage brush with the sand driving into your eyes, ears and mouth, being mixed in our dough, meat and coffee was a task that we seldom want repeated. We finally abandon the fire part and crouch into our wagons and nibble hard tack.

Nevertheless, she was impressed with a band of packers who knew how to have a hot meal in spite of the uncooperative weather:

> They got their coffee and bacon all right, one held his old hat over the fire while another an old black coffee pot and a frying pan partly grease and part sand. After straining the coffee through an old dish rag, had supper all right.[62]

When the emigrants reached the mostly barren Platte River Valley, the only fuel available was buffalo chips, a euphemism for the dried dung that covered the ground. Commenting on this fact, Nathan Putnam reflected that "I think with Col Russell that it is rather a hard matter that the Buffalo should furnish the meat and then the Fuel to Cook it with but nature seems to have so ordered."[63]

The chips burned well, and the overlanders who were experts at recycling, "picked up chips" and dropped them into their bags with hardly a grimace. E. W. Conyers describes one outing.

> Many of the ladies can be seen roaming over the prairie with sacks in hand, searching for a few buffalo chips to cook their evening meal. Some of the ladies are seen wearing gloves, but most of them have discarded their gloves and are gathering the buffalo chips with their bare hand.[64]

Gloves for gathering buffalo chips were not something they wished to carry to their new homes. Conyers noted that "the ladies have discarded for good their buffalo gloves." Although Conyers implies that only women gathered chips, it was really an equal-opportunity task. Everyone "picked up chips"; even youngsters got into the act. One can imagine the snickering and giggling among the youthful set when they heard a companion brag to his mother that he had found "some good fresh ones."[65]

Narcissa Whitman was the first of the overland women to lavish praise on the buffalo chip. She found it made a good fuel for cooking and was similar to the kind of coal used in Pennsylvania. Whitman wrote to her relations that she knew that when Harriet, her sister, read about eating a meal cooked over dung, she would "make up a face at this, but if she was here she would be glad to have her supper cooked at any rate."[66] As Amelia Hadley astutely observed, "It makes verry good fuel when dry, and is more prefforable than wood for the verry good reason, (can't get it)."[67] In some camps they called the best chip gatherer a "treasure."

If the chips were aged, the smell was minimal and did not flavor the food or scent the air too much. Fresh wet chips of course did not burn. Helen Carpenter speculated that after the chips lie on the ground for several years, the rains "wash away the objectionable parts and what remains is like *papier mache* and burns like punk."[68] (Punk, also called spunk or touchwood, is wood that has decayed from the action of a fungus.)

Carpenter and other overlanders used burning chips to drive pesky mosquitos from their wagons. Carpenter's method was typical: "When they are particularly troublesome in the day time a buffalo chip is lighted and placed in the wagon. This soon smokes them out. We can stand it longer than they can."

"GRASS IS USURPED BY THE ARTEMISIA"

Another source of fuel was mountain sage, or sagebrush (artemisia), which grew and still grows luxuriously in the Rocky Mountain states. In 1842, Captain Frémont noted in his journal that

Westward of Laramie river . . . the place of grass is usurped by the artemisia. . . . They grow everywhere—on the hills, and over the river bottoms, in tough, twisted, wiry clumps. . . . As the country increased in elevation on our advance to the west, they increased in size.[69]

There was so much sage that ten years later Amelia Hadley complained "that I cant bear to smell it."[70] Helen Carpenter noted that the water taken from a mud hole "did not lack much of being sage tea."[71]

Louisa Cook believed the sagewood resembled wormwood, reporting that it grew "about 2 ft high in bunches as large as a 1/2 bushel & the stalks about as large as a bean pole die down every year making very good fuel & indeed is all we have had to burn a good part of the time since we left the land of Buffalo Chips."[72] Wormwood actually is a species of artemisia; in fact, there are at least 180 species, according to *A Modern Herbal.* Artemisia is considered one of the most bitter plants in the world; "as bitter as wormwood" is an ancient proverb. Numerous species of artemisia are native to the temperate regions of Europe and Asia, but *Artemisia tridentata* is native to the western plains of the United States. The seeds are very oily, and the leaves are edible.[73]

The large sagebushes must have been a glorious sight as well as being aromatic. Charles Stanton compared its odor to lavender, but Captain Frémont and Margaret Frink detected the smell of turpentine mixed with camphor. Frink and her party were following Frémont's guide, so I suspect that she also followed Frémont's nose when she claimed that the sage smelled like "turpentine mixed with camphor."[74]

Both Charles Stanton and Amelia Hadley considered it "not like garden sage." But Elizabeth Smith sent word to her family that if they wanted to know how it burned, "jest step out and pull a lot of sage out of your garden and build a fire in the wind and bake boil and fry by it and then you will guess how we have to doo."[75] Smith did emphasize that it made a good fuel.

Were the plants that smelled like lavender and turpentine the same plant? It is hard to know. Amelia Hadley named many different plants growing in that area. "We see almost all kinds of plants and roots that grow in our garden and green houses of which is Cactus 2 kinds, Prickely Pear, Wormwood, Southernwood and Chamoile and an abundance of sage of which the latter is not like our garden sage."

The culinary sage (*Salvia officinalis*) that the emigrants grew in their gardens at home, and which we grow in ours, belongs to the genus *Salvia* and is not native to this country. It was imported from the Mediterranean. Those emigrants who said the sagebrush was not like garden sage were correct. Yet if the families at home had tried to burn their garden sage as Elizabeth Smith suggested, they would have had the same results as the emigrants had. Culinary sage is of course edible.

Also taking up space and scenting the air was a shrub called greasewood (*Sarcobatus vermiculatus*). According to Edwin Bryant, "In places [it] disputes the occupancy of the soil with the wild sage."[76] Bryant described greasewood "as three feet in height, with a bright green foliage containing a fetid, oily substance." Amelia Hadley compared it to a gooseberry bush but added that "the leaves look like hemlock."[77] Greasewood was also used as fuel: "Had good grass sage and greece wood for fuel," reported Susan Cranston.

BUILDING AN OVEN

Making an oven to burn the chips, sage, or even green wood required some ingenuity. Reuben Shaw in his reminiscences explained how his party managed to create an air tunnel that would provide a draft. The ramrod he used was a rod to drive home the charge of a muzzleloading gun.

A hole about six inches in diameter and eight to twelve inches deep was excavated. An air tunnel was then formed by forcing a ramrod horizontally from the river bank to the bottom of the cavity, giving the oven the required draught. In making a fire . . . a wisp of dry grass was lighted and placed at the bottom of the oven, opposite the air tunnel, feeding the flames with finely pulverized dry chips, which readily ignited.[78]

Shaw was burning buffalo chips and was amazed that "only a slight odor emitted from the fire." He was surprised "that the prejudice entertained against buffalo chips as a fuel had vanished into thin air." Lodisa Frizzell, who initially had entertained some doubts, seconded his opinion. She had "feared the dust would get in the meat, as it was frying." But when George (her husband) agreed to have his broiled, "laughing & joking we forgot our antipathies to the fire some said it had improved all the supper, even the coffee."[79]

Others did not bother with making a tunnel but relied on prevailing winds to create a draft. Charles Parke, a doctor, described the procedure for making a temporary oven.

An oblong hole is dug in the ground, say 18 inches long 8 inches wide and 6 inches deep. . . . The end of the oven is always facing to wind, consequently a fine draft is created. Simple, economical, and yet so perfect and practical. Better than a stove for a frontiersman. 'Tis always on hand and doesn't have to be transported.[80]

The Shaw party set rocks in their oven as a platform to hold the cooking pots; Charles Parke banked the sides of the makeshift oven with about four inches of sod and placed the kettle and frying pan on top. "The fuel, rosinweed, 'buffalo chips'—dried manure—or wood, is placed in the open oven and lighted." Louisa Cook's family "digs a little short trench in the ground just wide enough to let the frying pans & camp kettles rest on the edge."[81] Cook preferred this method to cooking on a stove. It took two to three bushels of dung to make a good fire and cook a meal, but buffalo chips and sage heated quickly.

STOVES: "THERE WERE PLENTY OF THEM"

Journal entries indicate that many pioneers followed Joel Palmer's advice and packed a stove. To facilitate transporting it Palmer suggested building a platform at the back of the wagon and storing it there. He emphasized that a stove would be convenient because "there is often a scarcity of wood."[82] Palmer never hinted at the kind of fuel that would work best.

"Most every family or mess in our train had a tent and sheet-iron cook stove," wrote P. H. Rountree of Lewis County, Washington.[83] "I also got a sheet-iron stove . . . which proved a real luxury as we were able to have warm biscuits for breakfast . . . besides many other delicacies which we could not have had by a campfire," recalled James Longmire.[84] "We got supper on our new stoves and had the first good bread we have had since we ate up what we baked before we left home. . . . We couldn't have done any cooking if we hadn't had stoves," confided Ruth Shackleford.[85] Other families had similar tales and wrote home that their stoves were invaluable and well worth the money. In a letter to his friends in Wisconsin, S. H. Taylor described the best type of stove to carry:

That which I believe is pronounced the best form of stove, is that of the common plate stove, but level at top and bottom, with two holes over the furnace, draught under and over the oven, and flue in the end. 3 or 4 feet perpen-

Two-step cooking stove (ca. 1850), built by Sherman S. Jewett & Company, Buffalo, New York (photographer, Steve A. Anderson).

dicular draught is necessary. We see none such among the hundreds that are thrown away. A stove should be double where most exposed to heat—say half the front end and bottom . . . Russia is the only sheet iron, that, in the stove will last through."[86]

If a stove was not available, Taylor suggested using "a sheet of iron like a stove top, to be put over a fire hole in the ground, a common means of cooking. . . . It is just as good as a stove for every purpose but baking."

Prices for stoves varied, depending on the type and on where and when it was purchased. In 1853 Welborn Beeson's family in La Salle County, Illinois, paid sixteen dollars for theirs; the Longmires in 1853 purchased one in Indiana for twelve dollars. In 1854 a sheet-iron cookstove was advertised for sale in St. Joseph for five dollars. Local newspapers carried ads for stoves along with other goods.

By the time the emigrants began their travels, major improvements in the technology of cast iron had made possible the extensive manufacture of cookstoves. Factories and foundries up and down the East Coast, particularly in Albany and Troy, New York, produced a wide variety of these new designs. From 1834 to 1837, 100 patents were granted for improvements in cooking stoves. Trade catalogs of the period proclaim that all new cookstoves and ranges incorporated the latest functions. The James Stove and the Rathbone Stove Works became household names in the 1830s as city families abandoned the fireplace for this more convenient method. W. T. James is credited with patenting the earliest cookstove in America.

The first cookstoves were in the form of a box stove, a plain box with cooking holes and a firebox. The first improvement added an oven with a door "which was in front and directly over the door for supplying fuel—and having also a boiler-hole and boiler on the back part of the top near the pipe."[87] An 1836 advertisement describes the Rathbone cooking stove as having "three boilers almost directly over the fire at once, and the improvement of the air flue between the oven and fire room, causes the oven to heat very equally and perfect."[88] The emigrants had their choice of several styles. Two period stoves that are now on display at the Oregon Trail Interpretive Center in Baker City, Oregon, show a difference in height, width, depth, and length. One, a "step stove," is thirty-six inches high and thirty inches wide; the other, box-shaped, is twenty-three inches high and twenty-four inches wide.

The Russia sheet iron that Taylor recommended was manufactured in Russia and was remarkable for its smooth, glassy surface. Its major characteristic was a "mirrow-like glaze of a smoky-grey colour," different from the bluish gray of common sheet iron. A screen of Russia iron placed in back of a stove reflected a great deal of heat into a room.[89] Russia sheet iron was listed in an 1851 advertisement that appeared in the *St. Joseph Gazette*.

STOVES: "I NEVER SHOULD THINK OF TAKING ONE"

Stoves, however, made up a large portion of the items left by the side of the road. Lucy Cooke expected to see the trail covered with a variety of goods, "but we saw but little that was of any good excepting stoves & there were plenty of them."[90] Cooke preferred a campfire: "I never should think of taking one as a bakeoven like yours [her sister's] with frying pan & iron pot, to cook out of doors is far preferable to a stove." And although Lodisa Frizzell used an abandoned stove for one night, she "then left it; for they are of very little account, unless you could have dry wood."[91] Actually, the overlanders used chips and sagebrush as well as wood in their stoves. Ruth Shackleford considered sagebrush "the best kind of stove wood."[92] Capt. David De Wolf assured his wife that "the darn stuff [buffalo chips] burns fine in a stove for I'd have you know we have a cooking stove."[93]

When Margaret Frink abandoned her stove after a collision with another wagon, she reached the same conclusion as

Force & Brown

Dealers in Stoves, and Manufacturers of Tin, Sheet Iron, and Copper Ware,

HAVE constantly on hand COOKING STOVES of all descriptions, Parlor and Air Tight Stoves, Sheet Iron Stoves,

Heating and Box do.
Seven and 10 plate do
Russia Sheet Iron do
Camp Kettles,
Block Tin,
Russia do
Sheet Lead,
 " Zinc,
 " Copper,
Tin Plate.

Also, a general assortment of Japaned and Hollow Ware, at Wholesale or Retail for Cash or approved paper, at the lowest market prices.

Messrs. Force and Brown hope by strict attention to business, and good work, to merit a share of public patronage.

Country Merchants and the public in general are respectfully solicited to call and examine our stock before purchasing elsewhere.

☞Our house is on Main street, sign of the Cooking Stove, and in the room recently occupied by J. & T. Curd.

St. Joseph, June 4, 1851.

Advertisement for Force and Brown. *St. Joseph Gazette* (ca. February 25, 1852). Courtesy of the State Historical Society of Missouri, Columbia.

Cooke and Frizzell—cooking over an open fire worked best. It is hard to imagine a "fender bender" happening on the wide-open plains, but Frink's accident report leaves no doubt about the crash:

> It being light, we had always carried it lashed on the hind end of the wagon. Some careless person, in a hurry, drove his team up too close behind, and the pole of his wagon ran into the stove, smashing and ruining it. After that, we had to cook in the open air. We adopted a plan which was very fashionable on the plains. We would excavate a narrow trench in the ground, a foot deep and three feet long, in which we built the fire. The cooking vessels were set over this, and upon trial we found it a very good substitute for a stove.[94]

Remember that in the year 1850, 50,000 persons were on the road to the West. White-topped wagons were everywhere and everyone had to travel during late spring and summer in order to avoid the early snow in the mountains and to be in their new homes before winter.

"LUCIFERS"

After gathering the fuel and preparing the oven, only one chore remained—starting a fire. For the emigrants who made the trek in the early years, this was a difficult task. Because of shipping and manufacturing problems, a cheap, plentiful supply of matches was not available. "Our matches, in a large-mouthed bottle were carefully guarded," Catherine Haun noted in 1849.[95] Borrowing fire from one's neighbor was common practice. If there were no matches and if the neighbors had no fire, then the emigrants would attempt a dangerous but quick way to start a fire. Jesse Applegate, who in 1843 traveled with the first large group of emigrants, described their method. "A man would rub a cotton rag in powder and shoot out of a musket, or put it in the pan of a flintlock gun, and then explode the powder in the pan."[96] Another old-fashioned method was to use a "burning glass," a small, round piece of glass that looked like a magnifying glass. The heat from the sun would shine through the glass, eventually starting a fire.

The first friction matches were jokingly called Lucifers and had to be drawn through folded sandpaper before they would ignite. Later improvements created matches that worked on any rough surface. The newer version of friction matches were called locofocus (*locus*: place, *focus*: hearth) or strike-anywhere. The first U.S. patent for friction matches was awarded in 1836; in appearance they were similar to today's wooden matches.

The early matches were not trouble-free and so were slow to be taken up by the emigrants. The matches had a tendency to explode when jostled, gave off a disagreeable odor (the composition was phosphorous, chalk, glue, and sulphur), and would not strike when damp. "Warranted to stand all weather and every climate," advertised one merchant in St. Louis in 1850. Such claims to perfection went too far. Manufacturers were still working out problems of design—how to produce an article in quantity that also would be cheap enough to throw away after it was used. And there was the problem of the health of factory workers; phosphorous fumes are deadly. The earliest matches were hand-cut and hand-dipped, and match manufacturing did not become big business until after the Civil War. Safety matches, that is, matches that ignite only on the box they come in and are made without phosphorous, did not begin appearing until the 1860s.

CHAPTER 3

Considering the number of open fires and lightning storms on the prairie, one would think that fires would have been frequent. No doubt dresses caught fire as women went too near their open ovens, and sparks must have landed on children playing too close to glowing fires. But in the many diaries I have read, only a few writers complained about accidental fires. Was William Hoffman's wagon the only that had a fire from a lantern left burning? Probably not, but at least we have his account:

> Last night we had well nigh met with a serious accident, by having our family wagon set on fire. We had left a piece of candle burning a lantern suspended from the bow of a wagon the candle having burned to the socket set fire to the grease in the bottom of the lantern, and the heat burned off the leather string by which the lantern was suspended. It fell on the bed where three of our children were sleeping. It was timely discovered and but little injury was done.[97]

With the provision box loaded, the pots and pans seasoned and ready for use, the water cleared, and the fire roaring, the energetic emigrants in their wagon wheel kitchens were ready to bake, broil, and eat. Both experienced cooks and those novices who had never boiled water would soon excel in the art of cookery.

4

THE WAY THEY COOKED

I have done a washing, stewed apples, made pies and baked a rice pudding. . . . After [supper] made two loaves of bread . . . prepared potatoes and meats for breakfast . . . pretty tired.

—Charlotte Stearnes Pengra

Cooking was time-consuming and often lasted far into the night, just as Pengra noted in her diary.[1] Even with proper provisions and good utensils, cooking over a campfire or in a rambling wagon for months on end was not easy. What talent, skill, and plain ingenuity went into mixing a cup of flour with a small amount of saleratus to produce a loaf of light bread? How did a prairie pea become a pickle? How was a tin of preserved milk transformed into a blancmange?

The evidence from diaries and letters lends credence to the popular belief that the overlanders' menu centered on a repetitious, boring diet of bread, bacon, and dried apples. Although the usual meal was not something a future cookery writer would want to include in "Best Recipes of the Overland Trail," not every meal consisted of monotonous fare. There were days of good eating. The diaries reveal that when the weather cooperated and fuel and water were available, the exuberant trail cooks, just like their counterparts at home, might experiment with a new way of preparing bread or making dried-apple pie. Catherine Haun, who made the trip as a young bride, recalled "exchanging recipes for cooking beans or dried apples or swapping food for the sake of variety."[2] Gradually, as the overlanders learned to bake and broil over an open fire, flavorful dishes simmered and bubbled in the versatile Dutch oven. New tastes and smells emerged from the crackling fire as each cook added a favorite ingredient to the day's recipe.

The overlanders managed to add the aroma of culinary creations to the sights and sounds of the prairies and plains because they had remembered to tuck a bit of Yankee ingenuity into the all-purpose provision box. These intangible supplies were certainly as important as flour and bacon for the emigrant who had to be concerned with cooking on the journey across the continent. On the trail many imaginative overlanders became skillful cooks as they adapted recipes and used available foods in order to feed their families. The ability to adapt or to substitute often made the difference between having a meal or going hungry, between eating boring salt pork or a sizzling hot sausage.

Content and satisfied with a Spartan diet of a "dry piece of bread & a tin cup of coffee," Louisa Cook chastised her sister for "grumbling if your biscuits werent light enough your coffee sweetened too much or not enough." But Louisa was exceedingly happy to have "a meal of warm pancakes bacon applesauce & tea with a hearty relish."[3] Abigail Scott, who boasted that she could "eat anything cooked almost any way . . . a peice of bacon placed between two peices of bread actually tastes better than the best of cakes and pies at home," sounded pleased when the menu for supper included "a fine dish of pheasants." Even a bachelor who admitted eating "bacon with fat 4 inches thick I can eat raw or fried" was overjoyed at the opportunity to have a proper meal that included "Liver, Ham, Coffee, Milk, Molasses, good light bread, biscuit, pickles & butter."[4]

In a series of letters to the *St. Louis Reveille*, George L. Curry, who traveled west in 1846, pointed out that the emigrants accepted boring edibles but delighted in a momentary gastronomic repast.

> Life on the plains far surpasses my expectation. . . . Bacon and hard biscuit may occasionally interfere with his *fairydom*, but that only occurs twice a day, and the influence is but momentary. To-day we have ripe strawberries upon the prairies—-we eat them with cream too, at that; think of it, and "begrudge" us.

> We supped last night on curlew, snipe, plover and duck—that's a prairie bill of fare for you! Don't your mouths water?—but they need not, if you let your minds take in the idea of the number of mornings and nights that plain middling meat, crackers and heavy biscuit comprise our fare.[5]

ADAPTING AND SUBSTITUTING

Among the first cooks to adapt and substitute ingredients in the standard European traveler's cuisine of the nineteenth century were Meriwether Lewis and William Clark, the first official explorers to approach Oregon country by the overland route. In 1803, almost forty years before wagon wheels began to leave their tracks beside the Platte River, Lewis and Clark recorded their instructions for preparing sausage from a newly killed buffalo cow. Their cook, the Canadian trapper Toussaint Charbonneau, prepared this delicacy. There in the wilds of today's middle America, Lewis and Clark adapted an ancient recipe for sausages. Not bothering to give the recipe a clever name, they called their dish *boudin* (*poudinque*) *blanc* and said, "This white pudding we all esteem one of the greatest del[ic]acies of the forrest." Forty years later, Captain Frémont, on an expedition to the West Coast, reiterated that praise: "The hunters came in with a fat [buffalo] cow; and as we had labored hard, we enjoyed well a supper of roasted ribs and *boudins*, the chef d'oeuvre of a prairie cook."[6]

Boudin is the French name for sausage; traditionally there are white and red sausages. Both are made from ground pork enclosed in a casing. The red sausage contained blood as well as meat; the white is made from white pork meat and fat. Onions, extra fat, seasonings, and butter are added to the mixture for flavor. Fortunately for us, Lewis thought "it may not be amiss therefore to give [the recipe] a place." The recipe with its detailed instructions is intriguing, the language evocative:

About 6 feet of the lower extremity of the large gut of the Buffaloe is the first mo[r]sel that the cook makes love to, this he holds fast at one end with the right hand, while with the forefinger and thumb of the left he gently compresses it, and discharges what he says *is not good to eat*, but of which in the s[e]quel we get a moderate portion; the mustle lying underneath the shoulder blade next to the back, and fillets are next saught, these are needed up very fine with a good portion of kidney suit [suet]; to this composition is then added a just proportion of pepper and salt and a small quantity of flour; thus far advanced, our skilful op-porater C——o seizes his recepticle, which has never once touched the water, for that would intirely distroy the regular order of the whole procedure; you will not forget that the side you now see is that covered with a good coat of fat provided the anamal be in good order; the operator sceizes the recepticle I say, and tying it fast at one end turns it inward and begins now with repeated evolutions of the hand and arm, and a brisk motion of the finger and thumb to put in what he says is *bon pour manger*; thus by stuffing and compressing he soon distends the recepticle to the utmost limmits of it's power of expansion, and in the course of it's longtudinal progress it drives from the other end of the recepticle a much larger portion of the [blank space in manuscript] than was prev[i]ously discharged by the finger and thumb of the left hand in a former part of the operation; thus when the sides of the recepticle are skilfully exchanged the outer for the iner, and all is compleatly filled with something good to eat, it is tyed at the other end, but not any cut off, for that would make the pattern too scant; it is then baptised in the missouri with two dips and a flirt, and bobbed into the kettle; from whence, after it be well boiled it is taken and fryed with bears oil untill it becomes brown, when it is ready to esswage the pangs of a keen appetite or such as travelers in the wilderness are seldom at a loss for.[7]

Boudin (*poudinque*) *blanc* was just one of the adapted dishes that emerged from the Overland Trail. The anecdotes and recipes that follow pay tribute to those capable cooks who traveled it and are part of the story of settling the West.

Taking along fresh dairy supplies presented problems, but circumstances at times provided solutions. We don't know who first realized that a day of wagon motion would turn milk to butter, but the method definitely caught on. Many of the pioneers remarked about that curious way of making butter. They would pour some milk in large jars, and the jostling of the wagons bouncing along a road pock-marked with ruts and grooves transformed the white liquid to butter "the size of a hickory nut and innumerable little ones like shot."[8] The leftover buttermilk provided a refreshing hot drink if the weather was warm and a cold one if the day turned cool. And "unlike the 'bean porrage' of school days, it is never 'nine days old,'" noted Helen Carpenter, showing her sense of humor.

If the wagon train did not travel with cows, the emigrants hoped to purchase butter in the jumping-off-towns, at trading posts, or from itinerant peddlers. They were not always successful. In April 1849 a review of grocery prices in the *St. Joseph Gazette* reported that the supply of butter was rather "limited and demand brisk"; it was selling for eighteen to twenty cents per pound. In that same year, taking advantage of the increased demand, a Mormon family raised cows in order to sell butter, milk, and cheese to emigrants. "They were evidently making money," reported Jasper Hixon.[9] By 1851 an ad in the *St. Joseph Gazette* offered butter for sale, but no price was given. In 1853 in Salt Lake City it was a scarce commodity. Lucy Cooke comments on her purchase of butter priced at thirty cents per pound:

> I have now got 5 lbs of butter which is as choice as gold I got it of our folks when we left them I should not have got it but I had a new pair of leather shoes I bought in the valley for $3 as one of their women

folks was most barefoot. they were glad to get them so paid me 1/2 in butter at 30 cents pr lb it was a mutual accomodation for I did not need the shoes.[10]

Cooke does not say how long the butter lasted or how she kept it fresh, but that must have been a problem since the emigrants traveled during the summer months. A makeshift ice box was worthless; any food in it would soon be swimming in warm water. The best procedure was to follow Eliza Leslie's directions to pack the butter down tightly in a jar and preserve it under a brine of "fine salt dissolved in water." Sallie Hester in 1849 mentions that their party started out with "packed butter." Randolph Marcy's guidebook, *The Prairie Traveler*, suggested "boiling it thoroughly, and skimming off the scum as it rises to the top until it is quite clear like oil. It is then placed in tin canisters and soldered up." The emigrants probably punched holes in the top of the canister and poured out the butter. Possibly they used a can opener; by 1859 usable can openers were available, the first U.S. patents having been granted in 1858.

Canned goods first came on the market in America when a patent for preserving foods in "vessels of tin or glass" was issued to Thomas Kensett and Ezra Daggett in 1825. One competitor, William Underwood, gained fame with tins of deviled ham. Still, not too many cans showed up in the marketplace because making them was a time-consuming process. Each top and bottom had to be cut individually by a skilled tinsmith and then soldered by hand to the can. In the canning process, food was put into the can through a small hole that had been cut in the top. Then a liquid was poured in and a small tin plate with a pin hole was soldered on. The can was boiled until steam escaped through the pinhole, at which time a drop of solder was placed over the hole. To make the can easy to open, manufacturers fastened a metal wire or a thin metal strip onto the lid. The strip was pulled to break the solder that sealed the lid.[11] Producing sixty "hole and cap" cans a day was considered a good output; canning was a labor-intensive industry.

The problem of slow production was solved in 1849 when Henry Evans invented a machine for pressing out the tops and bottoms of cans, increasing the output of cans from 120 to 1,500 per day in the early 1850s. Foods processed in tin cans became available to everyone. By the time the pioneers were trekking westward, tins of salmon, oysters, corn, tomatoes, and peas were being canned commercially. In 1853 Martin's grocery store frequently advertised in the *St. Joseph Gazette*, "Oysters, Lobsters, and Sardines for sale cheap." If only the cans had not been so heavy—with weight and space at a premium on the prairie schooners, there was room for only one or two specialties. Delicacies preserved in tins were a treat: "We lunched on canned peaches, then retired. Peaches were never more relished," a satisfied Ellen Tootle reported.[12]

A BLESSING AND A NUISANCE

In order to have fresh milk, many emigrants took along cows, a blessing for the fresh milk but a nuisance because often there was not enough feed or fresh water (cows had to be watched to prevent them from drinking strong alkali water). Jason Lee, a Methodist missionary, receives the credit for bringing the first cows overland to Oregon Territory. His cows were purchased in Liberty, Missouri, in 1834; two survived the trip. Lee did not indicate how many cows he started with, but he did comment that "the

Advertisement for Martin's Groceries. *St. Joseph Gazette* (ca. April 1853). Courtesy of the State Historical Society of Missouri, Columbia.

quart of milk which they afford us *now* per day is a small compensation for this labour but we hope to reap much benefit from them hereafter."[13] Although every year brought different experiences for the emigrants, the arduous task of watching over cattle was best expressed by Martha Read, who traveled to Oregon Territory in 1852:

> There was so much emigration before us that their teams eat up the feed so that we found but little food for our teams the latter part of our journey in particular so that we had to make short drives in order to save our teams there were a great many lost all their teams: some by over-driving and not having foot care and a great many died with the horn oil and some by drinking alchalye. it wants a great deal of care and attention to dumb beasts on this long journey. we counted over 600 dead cattle.[14]

In 1852 countless cattle died from disease, probably anthrax or "murrain." Horn oil or "hollow horn," which Read and others thought caused disease, was based on an old wives' tale that had its origin in the mistaken belief that "loss of appetitie and listlessness in a cow was due to 'hollow horns.'" To cure the cattle, emigrants filled the hole in the horn with salt, pepper, and sugar and plugged it with a wooden peg. The remedy was worthless.

The questions of whether to take cows along and whether young or old cows were better at making the journey were endlessly debated. Besides providing milk, and meat in a pinch, the cows were worth a lot of money in the new territories. In a letter to his hometown newspaper, Jerome Howard, who in 1849 was traveling to the goldfields, made a good case for bringing a milk cow.

Milk, cream, butter, cheese!—what meal can be perfect without them! I believe I recalled the honest
countenances of every cow my father ever owned,
since I was large enough to drive them to pasture;
deeply regretting every stone I ever threw at them, to
get them started from the field and every kick I ever
inflicted to make them "So!" Mr. Editor, have you a
cow! If so, give her in summer good pasture; and in
winter plenty of good hay and the choicest cabbage
stumps you can command; for she will well repay you:
and if you ever take an overland trip to California,
you will, while craving her precious products, receive
a special consolation for doing![15]

Jessy Lorney argued for bringing loose cattle but not
calves. Calves, he advised, "will not come through, and by
losing them you will be in danger of losing their moth-
ers."[16] Taking the opposite view, Peter Burnett "found
that yearling calves, and even sucking calves, stood the
trip very well."[17] If they could afford a few milk cows, emigrants started out with them. "See teams & cattle for 4 or
5 miles in length. This world is all a cattle show, sure
enough," Mary Burrell declared.[18]

For Helen Carpenter fresh milk became a staple as
she and her family would often have just bread and milk
for their noon meal. Other emigrants professed the same
story and added that milk was useful for softening dried
bread and stirring into coffee. We can speculate that innovative cooks added a few fresh berries to the milk and
made milkshakes, taking advantage of the bumpy wagon
ride for the shaking. Hannah King, from an upper-class
English family on the way to the Mormon settlement in
Utah, even used the milk for making a syllabub, a popular
English drink made from sweetened milk and wine and

sometimes eggs. We know that the King party had the necessary ingredients for this unusual trail drink because several days earlier they had toasted the Fourth of July with a glass of port. And they were traveling with milk cows. As for the eggs, we can only speculate. Two months earlier, on the morning they left Iowa for Utah, Hannah King had prepared "eggs beaten up with wine and Brandy." The chances of eggs surviving two months of bouncing and shaking were slim, however, and the Kings do not mention purchasing eggs along the way when they "went to a store [June 7] and bought a few things that we needed."[19] It would be interesting to know if King added fresh milk to the bowl in the manner suggested by Eliza Leslie. This recipe does not call for eggs.

COUNTRY SYLLABUB

Mix half a pound of white sugar with a pint of fine sweet cider, or of white wine; and grate in a nutmeg. Prepare them in a large bowl, just before milking time. Then let it be taken to the cow, and have about three pints milked into it; stirring occasionally with a spoon. Let it be eaten before the froth subsides.

During the emigration years, inventive manufacturers sought to eliminate the problem of trying to keep milk and butter fresh. Experiments for preserving milk began during this period, and a brief news item from *Scientific American*, May, 29, 1852, describes one process:

Various plans have been brought forward . . . for keeping milk in a fit state, at least for drinking with coffee and tea.

Milk has been preserved in the following manner. Fresh milk is reduced by boiling to one-half, and beaten with yolk of eggs, in the proportion of 8 eggs to every 10 and 1/2 quarts of milk. The whole is then placed on the fire for half an hour and skimmed frequently; it is next strained and heated in a waterbath for two hours. It is stated that this milk will keep good for two years, and if churned would afford good butter.

The process of preserving milk was perfected by Gail Borden, whose product became the popular condensed milk. By 1860 a factory in New York was capable of producing five thousand gallons of condensed milk per day. During the Civil War Borden's preserved milk was used by the army and navy.

On the trails the preserved milk was used in 1853 by Solomon Carvalho, the official photographer on Capt. John Frémont's fifth expedition. In preparation for his journey, Carvalho had purchased in New York "half a dozen cases of Alden's preserved coffee, eggs, cocoa, cream, and milk, which he sent out for the purpose of testing their qualities." According to Carvalho, the milk at least was of good quality:

I had reserved with religious care, two boxes containing one pound each, of Alden's preserved eggs and milk. (The yolks of the eggs were beaten to a thick paste with a pound of loaf sugar, the milk was also prepared with powdered sugar), and hermetically sealed in tin cases. . . . Nobody knew I had them. A paper of arrow root, which my wife had placed in my trunk, for diet, in case I was sick, I had also reserved. These three combestibles, boiled in six gallons of water, made as fine a blancmange mange as ever was

manged on Mount Blancmange. This "dessert" I prepared without the knowledge of Col. Frémont.

... the satisfaction and astonishment of the
whole party cannot be portrayed, when I introduced,
as dessert, my incomparable blancmange mange.
"Six gallons of *bona fide*," nourishing food, sweetened and flavored! It is hardly necessary to say, that
it disappeared in double quick time.[20]

A MESS OF GREENS

Indispensable for adding a dash of flavor and more than a
pinch of nutrients, wild greens were picked with pleasure
by the emigrants, who sorely missed having fresh food to
eat and who were aware that eating fresh vegetables prevented scurvy. The addition of onions, garlic, and dande-
lion or mustard greens to the soup pot makes a tasty, seasoned broth. Salty meat and dry biscuits stirred with a
few onions and perhaps a "mess" of mustard greens undoubtedly received a four-star rating from hungry people.
Food writers tell us the flavors "marry well."

In 1859 when George Keller set out to seek his fortune in the West, he reported that "provisions becoming
rather *scarce*, and we began using as a *substitute*, a weed
or 'greens' that is very abundant. Though not as *nutritious* as a great many other things, we could at least 'fill
up' on it."[21] Keller does not indicate what type of greens
he was using, but he does include a sort of recipe for his
soup and dumplings. Typical of inexperienced recipe writers, he forgot to mention the amount of greens added to
the pot:

The following scene will give the reader an idea of our
financiering in cookery. A. Clark, M. Hoover, and *our-*

self were cooking for ourselves and eleven others belonging to the mess. Our stock of provisions, consisted of a lot of musty tea, a few pounds of flour and a few dried elder berries. Hoover made the tea, while Clark and I made the *soup* and *dumplings,*—the preparations of the latter articles, being by *experimental philosophy,* deemed the most economical method of disposing of the flour. A handful of the berries were put into two camp kettles holding about six gallons of water. These gave *color* and *consistency* to the soup. A small quantity of flour was then made into a stiff batter. This was carefully divided by a spoon into a certain number of pieces, corresponding to the number of individuals in the mess.

The result of this *ceremony* was always announced in order that each one might learn, the amount of his share. I suppose any one might have eaten the entire amount, of course excluding a portion of the six gallons of tasteless soup.

When Alonzo Delano and his companions realized that the pink flowers they were gathering for nosegays were "wild chives, of an excellent quality . . . the nosegays were thrown aside and a supply of this member of the onion family were gathered for the evening meal."[22] Lucretia Epperson and her friend Mrs. Coleman were no doubt pleased with themselves when they found enough mustard greens to "make a good mess for supper. It was quite a treat to us, who had been so long without vegetables."[23] Mustard greens are also a good antiscorbutic since a cupful contains 67 milligrams of ascorbic acid (vitamin C), about the same amount contained in one medium orange. Epperson had found onions and cooked them for supper several days earlier; had she saved some of the onions and added them to the mustard greens for a two-vegetable meal?

Had Lucretia Epperson met Jean Baker along the trail she and Baker would have agreed on the merits of cooked greens. Baker found "a quantity of red-root greens, which when boiled are quite as good as spinach." The greens were probably wild rhubarb (*Rumex*), sometimes called western dock, or Swiss chard (*Beta vulgaris*), plants that have reddish stems. Baker said there were plenty growing near a small lake.

Even artichokes turned up on one menu in 1849. But from Peter Decker's diary entry, "had artichokes for supper and felt unwell after," it is impossible to know if Decker was referring to the globe or to the Jerusalem artichoke (the tuber of a sunflower, *Helianthus tuberosus*) or whether the vegetable was fresh, pickled, canned, brought from home, purchased from a trading post, or found growing in a field.[24] My vote goes to the fresh Jerusalem artichoke because it stores well and is native to this country. Although not particularly popular, like the potato, it rated more name familiarity than the globe artichoke. Decker, who carried an orange that he hoarded for almost six weeks and who, until he decided to go West, had not "used meat of any kind (except fowl & fish) for ten years," apparently would have been interested in trying out different vegetables. The orange, unlike the artichoke, did not make Decker sick; he considered it a luxury.

Many of the greens were usually found growing in the fertile river bottoms near the campsites. The wild onions resembled "our set onions only they are tougher," claimed Martha Read after gathering a large amount by the Platte River.[25] "Large quantities of wild onions were gathered by many of our party today, and being cooked with their bacon, composed the vegetable portion of their evening meal," Edwin Bryant recorded in his journal; "their odor is rank, and any thing but agreeable."[26] On the other hand, John Zieber, who picked them from the Missouri River bottom, found them "excellent . . . perfectly white and grow to be ordinary size of what are called onion buttons."[27]

Hannah King's traveling companion, Lizzie, found "fat hen" growing along the trail.[28] Interestingly, fat hen was specified as one of the greens Capt. George Vancouver found growing in the Pacific Northwest in 1792. Vancouver wrote that wild orache was "vulgarly called fat hen by his men . . . and were considered by us as excellent of their kinds, and served to relish our salt provisions."[29] There is no explanation as to why orache is referred to as fat hen.

Kenneth Holmes states that fat hen is *Chenopodium alban* or "shepherd's purse"; orache has the scientific name *Atriplex hamilus*. Both plants have large leaves and are similar to spinach. The plant that Lizzie found may have been either. I grow orache in my garden and can verify that it imparts a flavorful taste to the soup pot; it is also good raw.

Prairie peas (*Thermopsisa*), growing on a leguminous vine that closely resembled the common pea vine but that produced peas about the size of a walnut, were also picked to perk up the pioneer's meals. Several journal writers in fact were intrigued to find this plant growing in the wild. George L. Curry best described this wonderful vegetable.

I took a skir[mish] among the hills yesterday, in hopes of finding buffalo, and discovered, among other things, . . . *green peas*. Just think of it, green peas in a hollow among the sand hills, miles away from the emigrant route. They resemble the cultivated pea in every respect, excepting that the leaf of the vine, or bush, is entirely different.[30]

Taking the advice of Joseph Ware, resourceful trail cooks turned the pea into pickles. Although Ware had recommended them in his guide as a food to be eaten in "times of scarcity," one of his party, a Mrs. Grayson, thought "they were equal if not superior to any delicacy of the kind which I have ever tasted."[31] Edwin Bryant, also with that group, described the prairie pea in detail.

The fruit has an agreeable taste, resembling that of the green pea of our gardens. In a raw state, it is eaten by travelers on the plains to quench thirst. It makes a most excellent pickle, as we afterwards discovered, scarcely inferior to the olive. . . . The plant which produces it is about eight inches in length, and has a leaf similar to that of the wild pea vine. The fruit, which varies from half an inch to an inch in diameter, has a tough rind, with a juicy pulp, the flavor of which resembles that of the green pea in its raw state. In the heart of the fruit there are a number of small seeds. Mrs. Grayson, having the necessary spices, &c, made of the prairie pea a jar of pickles, and they were equal if not superior to any delicacy of the kind which I have ever tasted.[32]

Francis Sawyer, who also made pickles from the prairie peas, concurred with Joseph Ware. "We picked some nice prairie peas to-day, but they cannot be considered as much of a luxury, as they are only good for making pickles."[33] The pickles were probably made by dropping the peas into a container of vinegar and spices and letting them "pickle" for a few days. Perhaps Mrs. Grayson's pickles were better than Sawyer's because she used better vinegar.

Thinking ahead to a time when the soup pot would need flavoring and anticipating that wild greens might not be growing along the trail, shrewd cooks dried the wild plants. In Mary Bailey's case, the dried herbs were bartered for meat. A doctor in a passing wagon saw a plant Mary called hogwort drying on her wagon and "offered me some mutton & called one of the boys & sent me a sheep."[34] The scientific name for hogwort is *Croton capitatus*, but in popular lore hogwort refers to any dried plant.

Although Inez Eugenia Adams Parker in her recollections suggested that there was a problem distinguishing "noxious plants from the innoxious," the plants referred to most frequently in the diaries are easily identified.[35] Perhaps the most significant feature of Parker's recollections is that she referred to her mother as a botanist. Very few women at that time had a descriptive professional adjective attached to their names.

"QUITE A DESSERT"

Scarcely any diary of a western crossing fails to mention the bonanza of finding luscious berries, such as wild grapes, currants, gooseberries, and strawberries. Like the fresh greens, they were a culinary delight and a luxurious substitute for dried fruit. The crown jewels of campfire cuisine, berries made a meal memorable by brightening the daily fare of bacon and beans. The women served them for tea where "they relished well" and turned the succulent berries into jams and pies. When the overlanders found strawberries and if the cows were still producing milk, a special treat of strawberries and cream was served. The surplus berries were dried for later use. Mary Rockwood Powers boasted that she had made dumplings from her stock of dried strawberries.

> When we came to the last camp before we parted, I took the last of my dried strawberries and stewed them, and wet up some light dough and rolled it out with a bottle and spread the strawberries over it, and then rolled it up in a cloth and boiled it, and then with the juice of the strawberries and a little sugar, and the last bit of nutmeg I had made quite a cup full of sauce to eat upon the dumplings. . . . The dumplings were light as a cork and made quite a dessert.[36]

If the emigrants had milk or eggs, which they occasionally were able to purchase from itinerant peddlers, innovative cooks such as Mary Burrell could make currant pudding. Eleven days earlier, while camped near Salt Lake City, Burrell's company had been approached by an old woman who wanted to trade butter, cheese, and eggs for groceries or old clothes. Burrell writes that they bought cheese but does not indicate if they traded for eggs.[37] Nineteenth-century cookbook writers usually included several recipes for puddings without eggs in their cookbooks.

Finishing a meal with "pudding," according to popular nineteenth-century cookbooks, was an English custom that was brought to America. "In England where the fog is nearly perpetual, the stomach requires to be filled with something heavy, something that will stay there till the next meal," proclaimed Pierre Blot in 1868.[38] Certainly the same requirement applied to the emigrants, who expended thousands of calories as they marched west. Whatever the reason, perhaps chiefly because they tasted good, puddings were popular. Even an 1854 dietetic cookbook, which recommended low-fat and low-sugar foods, was forgiving when it came to puddings. Made of a mixture of rice or bread, milk, eggs, or fruit, puddings were boiled or were sometimes baked like pies, probably the method used on the trail. Making a boiled pudding was more complicated than baking one. The dough had to be wrapped in a floured cloth and placed in a container of boiling water to simmer for several hours. Cookery-book authors of course left elaborate directions for this process.

I have yet to find a diary that gives a recipe for making puddings on the trail, but period cookbooks listed several varieties of fruit puddings as well as rice, potato, curd, and nut puddings. The diarists often described the kind of pudding they prepared or named the ingredients, though. For instance, Lucy Cooke wrote, "We also got a nice piece of beef with some beautiful suet for puddings Wm being very fond of them."[39] Cooke may have followed a variation of these recipes.

A SUET PUDDING

Grate the soft part of a small loaf of bread, and mix with it three quarters of a pound of hard lumps of suet, that have been finely shred and sprinkled with a little salt, and two spoonfuls of flour. Boil a quart of sweet milk, pour it over the bread crumbs and suet; cover them and set them by till they get cool. In the meantime, prepare a large spoonful of mixed mace and nutmeg, a glass of mixed brandy and wine, and beat very light six fresh eggs. When the suet, &c. are cold, beat them together, stir in the spices and brandy, and then stir in the eggs. When the whole are very well commingled, put it in a pudding cloth, tie it securely, and boil it in the usual manner for all boiled puddings. Send it to table very warm.[40]

PUDDINGS WITHOUT EGGS

Very good puddings may be made *without eggs*; but they should have very little liquid added to them, and must boil longer than puddings with eggs. A spoonful of yeast will serve instead of 2 eggs, and a pinch of soda will make it still lighter. Two large spoonfuls of snow will supply the place of 1 egg and make a pudding equally good. . . . The sooner it is used after it falls the better; but it may be taken up from a clean spot, and kept in a cool place some hours, without losing its good qualities."[41]

Several varieties of currant berries flourished in the regions crossed by the overlanders. Eliza McAuley recalled finding a fragrant profusion of black, red, and white bushes, "some of them ten feet long and loaded with ripe currants, which we strip off and make into jelly, currant wine and vinegar, dried currants and currant pie."[42] Elizabeth Smith found yellow ones that she believed better "than tame currents," and described gooseberries as "smothe as currents and tasted much like fox grapes all the goose berries this side [west] of the Missouri is smothe." Fox grapes, *vitis labrusca*, grow on a hardy, woody vine that produces an edible, thick-skinned, sweet, musky berry. This is the origin of many American grape varieties. Whether Smith actually found currants and gooseberries is difficult to know because the two plants are easily confused. Both belong to the genus *Ribes*, both grow throughout North America, both show considerable variation in berry color, both have similar looking leaves, and many species have similar common names. As a rule, currants usually lack thorns and are generally smooth-skinned; gooseberries are many-seeded and bristly. But there are many exceptions and frequently only a botanist can specifically identify the native plants. Rich in pectin, currants were the perfect fruit for making jams and jel-lies.[43]

The currant pie recipe found in a reprint of an 1853 Quaker cookbook could have been prepared by the emi-grants without too much trouble. The gooseberry wine recipe is from an 1839 Kentucky cookbook. In this recipe the author did not specify the type of sugar, but in other fruit wines included in the same book, she called for loaf sugar.

CURRANT PIE

After steaming green currants, scald them, and allow them to stand a while; pour off the water; have the crust in your plates, put in the currants, sweeten them well; put in a little water, a dust of flour and a little orange peel. Gooseberries are prepared in the same way, but require more sugar.[44]

GOOSEBERRY WINE

Break up the ripe berries, press the juice through a sieve, to each five gallons of which add ten gallons of water, and thirty-five pounds of sugar. Ferment, and afterwards cork it up.[45]

Overlanders also gathered buffaloberries and haw-berries. Sophia Goodridge picked thirty-three quarts of buffaloberries, which she said "taste very much like cur-rants and are red. They have one seed in them and make very good sauce and pies."[46] Buffaloberry (*Shepherdia canadensis*) is named because Native Americans cooked the dried berries with buffalo meat when they prepared pemmican (from the Cree, *pemikân*), a food made from dried meat, berries, and melted fat. It was very nutritious and kept well. Fresh buffaloberries can be yellow, orange, or reddish.

Gathering berries not only added to the larder but served as a social event for the young people. Harriet Buckingham, nineteen years old and unmarried when she made the trip in 1851, provided this charming description of searching for berries:

> To day again we thought to try our fortune in berrying some of the young gentlemen of the camp went with us & taking each a pail & basket of hard bread & venison we started invoking the gods to be more propiteous for it was a long toilsome walk to climb the Rocky Mountan & then not to get one raspberry it was too bad though we did find wild currants & service berries but we were a merrie party. O it was so hard to climb—to jump from rock to rock sometimes swinging ourselves by holding a shrub & clinging to the roots after ascending about a mile, we . . . found a small spring . . . & were quite refreshed with a drink of ice water. Two miles brought us to the long sought [raspberries]. . . . I never saw larger ones cultivated in our gardens at home.[47]

When the emigrants neared the end of their journey and food supplies were almost nonexistent, berries, besides perking up dull meals, often assuaged the pangs of hunger. Abigail Scott's sister Etty remembered such days in the Cascade Mountains: "Our provisions were exhausted by this time and for three days we had only Salal berries, and some soup made by thickening water from flour shaken from a remaining flour sack." Etty was eleven years old when she traveled with her parents to Oregon Territory in 1852. Salal berries (*Gaultheria shallon*) are dark blue to black with numerous seeds, which give them a grainy texture. They are common in the Northwest and were popular among the Native Americans who ate the berries fresh in summer and dried them for winter use.

BAKE THAT BREAD

An impressive amount of cooking was accomplished during the four to six months of camping, and baking headed the list. Incredulous as it may seem, during the myriad of daily chores the cooks found time to prepare apple pies, mince pies, peach pies, pot pies, pumpkin pies, apple and strawberry dumplings, gingersnaps, fruit cakes, nut cakes, doughnuts, light bread (salt-rising), and sourdough bread.

Whether they were housekeeping at home or on the trail, most nineteenth-century women regularly baked bread and pies. Large cities had bakeries, but for the many people who still lived in farming communities, home-baked bread was the only bread available. For the emigrant cooks, at least for the women, baking bread was a task that many of them knew how to do. If, like Virginia Ivins and Catherine Haun, they did not, they quickly learned. Haun admitted that "having been reared in a slave state my culinary education had been neglected and I had yet to make my first cup of coffee." But when the woman hired to do the cooking left, "I surprised all by proposing to do the cooking, if everybody else would help." Her offer was accepted and "as quantity rather than quality was the chief requisite to satisfy our good appetites I got along very well."[48]

Virginia Ivins acknowledged that neither she nor the hired cook knew how to bake loaf bread, and everyone was "very tired of batter cakes and poor heavy biscuits." Then one evening they camped by a family baking bread, and she "took courage and called on my neighbor of the night to ask for information." The neighbor not only agreed to give breadbaking instructions but presented Ivins with a Dutch oven. "I did just as my kind neighbor directed and in the morning had two loaves of elegant bread." Ivins was surprised that "making little fires of sage twigs on the lid and under the oven" did any good, but "the bread came out a beautiful brown."[49] Undoubtedly there were other inexperienced cooks who quickly learned the art of baking bread and brewing a pot of coffee.

Experienced or not, emigrant cooks were not familiar with baking outdoors over buffalo dung with the wind blowing smoke in their faces. Regulating the fire to prevent burning the bread and having to put up with the ashes from the various types of kindling settling on the dough were among the biggest problems for these outdoor cooks.

Of course not everyone baked good bread. Charles Parke, traveling with a company of men longing for good homemade biscuits, persuaded a woman in another camp to cook for them. "In due time the long looked for morsels appeared from the Dutch oven smoking hot. . . . They could be scented afar off. Solid as lead. Oh, Lord, what a disappointment. Sorry for the poor woman. She thought they were splendid."[50] Prior to that encounter, Parke and his traveling companions believed that all women were better at baking than men.

For the people back home, bread was an addition to

the menu; for those on the trail, it was generally the only food available. At home, bread had time to rise; on the trail, the emigrants usually baked a quick bread. Quick bread or mountain bread was basically a mixture of flour and water, fried in buffalo grease or lard. If there was no bowl for mixing, the dough was stirred in the pan; at least that is how Elisha Perkins did it:

Having no pan was obliged to mix [dough] in a frying pan the iron of which gave it somewhat the color of rye bread succeeded however in producing some rather good cakes which at home would have been pronounced rather too full of ashes cinders &c to say nothing of the brown appearance of the inside, but which we thought quite nice.[51]

Proud of her culinary skills, Narcissa Whitman sent a recipe for fried cakes to her mother and sisters still at home in the East:

Girls, If you wish to know how they (fried cakes) taste, you can have the pleasure of taking a little flour & water & make some dough roll it thin, cut it into square blocks, then take some beef fat and fry them! You need not put either salt or pearl ash in your dough. Believe me I relish these as well as I ever did any made at home.[52]

The Farmer's and Emigrant's Handbook offered this version of a quick bread:

QUICK BISCUIT

One quart sour cream, a large tea-spoonful saleratus, a little salt, and flour enough to make a paste stiff enough to roll. This can be baked, in a spider on a few embers.

If you have some milk or buttermilk, you can make them very nice by rubbing a small bit of shortening into the flour and mixing with the milk as in the foregoing you use the cream.[53]

To show off their cooking skills, experts flipped the cakes by giving the frying pan a sudden lift and tossing the pancake into the air, then catching it on the other side as it landed in the pan. The grain in the pancakes was either flour or cornmeal. Diarists who mentioned that they were making Indian pancakes were using cornmeal.

Some emigrants made a quick bread called bread-on-a-stick. The dough, a mixture of flour and water, was prepared right in the flour sack. The cook then inserted a stick in the bag and scooped and twisted up some dough until it clung to the end. To bake the bread-on-a-stick, the stick with its glob of dough was stuck in the ground near the fire and from time to time turned to prevent burning.

A more substantial bread was made by adding saleratus to the flour and water, kneading this mixture, letting the bread rise, and then baking it in an old-fashioned skillet or Dutch oven. Emigrants referred to it as "light" or "lightnin' bread," a term for salt-rising bread, which used saleratus or baking powder as a leavening instead of yeast. The usual procedure was to mix the bread in the morning, allow it to rise during the day, and bake it in the evening when the wagon train stopped. Keturah Belknap reversed the procedure, but she at least left us a recipe of sorts; most of the letter writers and diarists recorded only a brief reference, such as "I set in tins & baked light bread—two nice loaves." As was usual with early culinary writers, Belknap made no mention of amounts:

> When I made bread I made "salt rising." When we camped I made rising and set it on the warm ground and it would be up about midnight. I'd get up and put it to sponge and in the morning the first thing I did was to mix the dough and put it in the oven and by the time we had breakfast it would be ready to bake; then we had nice coals and by the time I got things washed up and packed up and the horses were ready the bread would be done and we would go on our way rejoicing.[54]

Thanks to Phoebe Judson, who in her reminiscences was wise enough to realize that "as there are many girls and young wives who are not adepts in this simple art of the culinary department," we have a few measurements. Judson called this recipe old fashioned salt-rising:

PHOEBE JUDSON'S BREAD

To one quart of water, one teaspoon of salt, thickened with flour until a stiff batter; I then set the little bucket containing the yeast into the camp kettle (covering it tightly to keep out the dust) and letting it remain in the front part of the wagon where the sun kept it warm. The secret in making it rise was the part the oxen and wagon performed—in keeping it well stirred, or in constant motion. When we came to a halt at noon it was sure to be light and foaming over into the kettle. I then poured it into the bread pan, adding as much more water and thickened flour; when it again became light I kneaded it into a large loaf while the wagon was jogging along; when we reached our camping place at night my bread was ready to put into the "Dutch oven" and bake.

> By this method I never failed to bake as light and
> sweet bread as ever made by modern devices.[55]

Besides writing down her bread recipe, Judson described
several amusing breadbaking disasters. In one instance
she set the finished bread on the grass to cool and cleaned
up her wagon. Hearing the laughter of children, she
"glanced in that direction, and what was my dismay to
see little Annie standing on my precious loaf. I found that
she and little Alta Bryant had been having a most enjoyable time rolling it on the grass."

The other incident, as Judson put it, was even more
ludicrous. Mrs. Bryant, a companion on the trip, had "set
her sponge in the bread pan to rise and left it in the
wagon, where her little boy, less than two years old, was
sleeping, while she, with others, went for a short stroll.
When she returned to the wagon she found her little boy
in the bread pan, up to his knees in the dough." Although
it is easy for us to laugh at those events, given the time involved in baking bread, the pioneer women probably
wanted to sit down and cry.

The yeast in Judson's recipe was probably similar to a
sourdough starter or to a leavening agent the emigrants
called "emptings," a lump of dough that had been allowed
to ferment. Several early cookbooks and magazines offer
recipes for making a yeast to be used in baking what Keturah Belknap called "salt-rising" bread.

SALT RISING, OR YEAST

Make a quart of water lukewarm, stir into it a table-
spoonful of salt, and make it a tolerably thin batter
with flour; mix it well, sprinkle on the top a handful
of dry flour, and set it in a warm place to rise, but be
sure you do not let it get hot, or it would spoil it. Turn

it round occasionally, and in a few hours it will be light, and the top covered with bubbles; then make up your bread into rather a soft dough, adding as much lukewarm water as will be found necessary. . . . Bake as other light bread.[56]

Yeast in those years was not generally put up in small packages to be tucked in among the provision box; rather, the yeast used to bake bread at home was a bubbling mixture of flour, sugar, water, and hops or potatoes. It was put up in crocks or bottles and was dependent on the wild yeast that exists in the air to activate it. When that yeast came in contact with the sponge (the bubbling mixture of flour), it produced carbon dioxide, which made the bread rise. The yeast was most unstable—not something to carry on long journeys. In fact, nineteenth-century cookery writers often suggested adding baking soda or baking powder to bread recipes because they were not certain the homemade yeast would work. Culinary historians such as Waverly Root give 1868 as the year commercial yeast became available.

"SPIT IN MY EARS AND TELL ME LIES, BUT GIVE ME NO DRIED APPLE PIES"

Pies placed a close second in the baking department after bread. Apple pie headed the list, but mince, pumpkin, peach, currant, and pot pies were mentioned in diaries and letters. The fruit used was usually dried, except on days when someone gathered fresh berries. Fresh fruit was too heavy and too perishable to transport. Even though baking pies involved mixing dough, making a crust, stewing fruit, and lighting a fire, pies were such a part of the American cuisine that women were expected to make them for most meals. A spider or a Dutch oven made an excellent pie pan; pies could be fried or baked.

To make a fried pie the cook placed sweetened, stewed fruit on half a rolled-out pie crust, folded the other half of the crust over the fruit, and crimped the ends of the pastry together. The pie was then fried in hot shortening until it was brown on both sides. The cookery writer Lettice Bryan advised using the leftover shortening (she preferred butter) for gravies. But whether the pie was fried or baked, the trail cook had to figure out where to roll the dough and how to prevent the bottom crust from burning.

The main complaint about pies was their sameness. "Spit in my ears and tell me lies, but give me no dried apple pies" exemplifies only one of many ditties coined by the emigrants. Dried apples were not used just for apple pies but were added to savories. And Patty Sessions used them for making mince pies, saying that the practice "was fine for lunch." Perhaps the boredom with and dislike of dried apples were best expressed in this tale from *A History of Bellingham*. Mr. and Mrs. Lysle had come to Oregon Territory in 1854 but were beginning another move:

> Accordingly, in two canoes lashed together, they brought all their earthly possessions with household goods. Among these were a keg of candles and a keg of dried apples. Coming around an island a rough sea tipped the overloaded canoes, and Mr. Lysle, thinking only of the safety of the babies, pitched overboard the keg of candles. Mrs. Lysle grieved for months over their loss, bewailing the chance that it had not been the apples that were cast away.[57]

To roll out crusts, cooks used flat surfaces such as wagon seats, a board, or the top of the provision boxes. If a rolling pin was not available, resourceful cooks used a cup, a bottle, or their hands to shape the dough for the crust. Rather than a flaky crust, these pastry chefs hoped for a crust that would hold a filling and would not burn on the bottom when cooked over a quick-burning hot fire. Lard was the preferred shortening, although when that was not available, Lucy Cooke used tallow and was proud of it. "We bought a lump of tallow 25 cents pr lb this we use for *pie crust* & candles is it not handy."[58] Tallow, fat rendered from beef or mutton, is also used to make candles and soap. The absence of shortening meant a bland crust of flour, water, and salt. Fruit was air-dried and quite hard. Before it was put in the pie crust, the dried fruit was softened either by soaking it in hot water or simmering it over a fire.

Whether the pot pie baked by Elizabeth Austin resembled the dish we know today with a top and bottom crust enclosing a mixture of meat and vegetables is impossible to know. Recipes from a few old cookbooks of that period suggest that pot pies may have described a fricassee of meat with dumplings or the ever-present stew.[59] Actually, that method of preparation seems preferable; it was certainly easier for people baking over an outdoor fire to make a dumpling—a mixture of flour, a liquid (milk or water), and seasonings dropped into a steaming broth—than to roll out a crust.

Other baked goods written about in the diaries included apple dumplings, crulls (crullers), fruit cakes, doughnuts, fritters, fosnocks, bran dumplings, ginger snaps, fruit cakes, molasses cake, and cookies. Lodisa Frizzell made "crulls" with saleratus and sour milk, which she kept in a glass pickle jar, and then fried them. She declared that "I had as fine cakes as if I had been at home."[60] Crullers, popular Pennsylvania Dutch cake-style

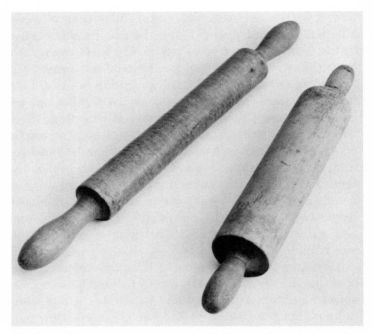

Wooden rolling pins (ca. 1790 and 1900); carved, turned wood. Courtesy of the Museum of History and Industry, Seattle, Washington, gifts of Mrs. Mildred M. Row and Mrs. Perry P. Hensley (photographer, Howard Giske).

doughnuts, also included sugar and eggs in the list of ingredients; sometimes mashed potatoes were used. The cakes were fried in hot fat.

The Pennsylvania Dutch popularized fosnocks (fastnachts) or doughnuts, different names and spellings for the same sweet. The Tuesday before Lent is "Fastnacht Day" in Pennsylvania Dutch country, and to ensure a healthy year, one eats fastnachts on that day. Traditionally, the fastnachts were rectangular, not round, and had a cross in the center instead of a hole. There is much debate as to whether they are better made with yeast or with baking powder. The ingredients, flour, sugar, milk, butter, eggs, and baking powder or yeast, are mixed together, the dough formed, and small portions cut out. The fastnachts are then dropped into hot fat to cook, removed and dipped in sugar, and served. James Hutchings enthusiastically recalled that when he returned to camp and saw the "fosnocks" they were "literally devoured."[61] Of course we do not know how the cook in Hutchings's camp prepared those goodies. He may have simply mixed some flour, sugar, and water, fried the sweet dough in oil, and then doused it with more sugar. But it is nice to know that there was food to get excited about.

Culinary historians give credit for the creation of the doughnut to the Pilgrims who reportedly learned to make these delicacies in Holland. But several legends credit other sources. In one story, Hanson Gregory, a Maine sea captain, was unhappy that his mother's fried cakes had a soggy middle. A typical son, he offered a better way and told his mother to leave out the center. An agreeable mother, she made the cake with a hole in the center. True or not, in 1947 a plaque was placed in the house where Gregory lived to honor the hundredth anniversary of the birth of the doughnut.

Another story attributes the origin of the doughnut to a seventeenth-century Nauset Native American. Legend has it that a young man playfully shot an arrow through a fried cake that a woman was making. She was frightened and dropped the perforated patty into a kettle of boiling grease. The delicacy that emerged was the doughnut.[62]

Ellen Tootle reported that when her party stopped in Nebraska City they were served fruit cakes, but she commented that the cakes were really molasses cakes with raisins. Several other women write about baking fruit cake; perhaps they too were talking about a molasses cake. Molasses was cheap and popular although not as convenient as sugar to carry. The overlanders certainly were not baking the traditional Christmas fruit cake that contains butter and brandy and that needs to be stored for several weeks while the flavors blend. That kind of cake did not lend itself to trail cooking, but the following recipes did. Nuts, raisins, and a variety of spices were available; an advertisement in an 1848 *St. Joseph Gazette* lists filberts, almonds, pecans, allspice, ginger, and nutmeg for sale. It was understood in those days that everyone knew how to bake a cake, and precise directions were not always included.

SUPERIOR MOLASSES GINGER-BREAD

Take two tea-cupfuls of molasses, one tea-cupful of butter, a table-spoonful of ginger, and two tea-spoonfuls saleratus and mix well. Bake quick.[63]

GOOD FRUIT CAKE WITHOUT EGGS

1½ cups brown sugar, 3 tablespoons butter, 1 cup sour milk with small teaspoon soda, 2 cups flour, 1 cup raisins, 1 cup nuts and spices, pinch salt.[64]

Homemade cookies were another flavorful treat that hardworking cooks managed to bake on the trail. "The boys steal them [cookies] as fast as she can bake them," complained seventeen-year-old Eliza McAuley.[65] But Eliza and her sister Margaret were having an easy day; they had traveled only six miles and were camped in a good area, and before the cookie-baking session they had had fun "making pop corn candy." McAuley doesn't tell us what kind of cookies the boys devoured, but Mary Burrell baked gingersnaps. She may have used a recipe similar to

this one from *The New England Economical Housekeeper,*
1847.

GINGER SNAPS

Boil a tea-cupful of molasses, and add two spoonfuls
of butter, one spoonful of ginger, and one tea-spoonful
of saleratus; stir the flour in when it is hot, roll it
thin, cut it in rounds. Bake quick.[66]

At seventy-eight, Catherine McDaniel Furniss fondly
recalled the days on the trail when her mother baked
cookies. She was eight years old when her family crossed
the plains.

Mother had been artist enough in cutting them out,
that we could pick out the different shapes. We cher-
ished our little cookies and were loth to eat them. But
finally we could not resist the temptation to take just
a wee taste; so few sweets did we get those days. We
would just take a bit of a nibble like mice. We would
try to make them last as long as possible.[67]

Commenting about the cut-out cookies, Jeanne Watson
speculates that Catherine's mother "outlined the animal
figures with a knife and then removed the excess dough
from the cookie sheet rather than using cookie cutters."
    One of the pluses I enjoyed in reading so many diaries
was discovering an atypical food item and trying to figure
out what that food was. On the day Cecelia Adams recorded her many cooking tasks, such as cooking beans
and baking pies, she added that she had made "dutch
cheese." Adams almost certainly was not preparing a type
of Edam or Gouda, popular Dutch cheeses, as these were
too complicated and too time-consuming to make at a

campsite. Her Dutch cheese instead referred to a thick cream cheese made without heat or rennet. The basic preparation involved putting thick cream in a linenlike bag and allowing the liquid to drip out. The thickened cream remaining in the bag was Dutch cheese. This was a popular, easy-to-make cheese among the Pennsylvania Dutch long before Philadelphia Cream Cheese appeared.[68]

"YOU COULD NOT TELL IT FROM BEEF"

By the time the wagon trains reached buffalo (bison) country, most of the emigrants longingly anticipated a meal of freshly cooked meat. Salted meat had its place, but it could not replace the fresh for weary travelers. The emigrants eagerly devoured the buffalo that had already been so generous in providing fuel for baking bread and cooking beans. The enticing fresh meat with its assertive flavor was just what they thought they wanted. Peter Burnett's description of a meal of buffalo might rival restaurant reviews in the *New York Times*:

> Mrs. B. had six large slices of this meat cooked for me. I supposed I could eat three of them, as I thought they would be sufficient for any one; but when I had eaten them, I felt a strong inclination to eat the fourth, and so I eat them all. About two hours afterward, supper came on, and we had more of this fine meat. Doctor Long took supper with me, and something was said about Oregon. The Doctor remarked, that he feared Oregon was like the buffalo meat, overrated. Said I, "Doctor, I have always thought as you do in regard to buffalo meat until this day, and now I think it has always been underrated." . . . From this you may infer

that I was a gormandizer; but if I can judge impartially, in my own case, I assure you, I was not more so than most persons on the road.[69]

Other testimonies from pleased diners indicate that after indulging in this gastronomic treat, almost everyone became an instant aficionado. "I think there is no beef in the world equal to a fine buffalo cow—such flavor so rich, so juicy, it makes the mouth water to think of it," noted Charles Stanton.[70] "A fat buffalow heifer is as good meat as I would wish to taste of," emphasized. Elizabeth Dixon Smith.[71] "It is a very coarse and dark meat but when cooked right made a very good change," according to Keturah Belknap. "We had been confined to salt meat for several weeks; and were prepared to do ample justice to a dish of steak—being unanimous in our verdict that the meat was excellent. We salted a small quantity for the future, not knowing how to jerk it as is usually done," reported Samuel Dundass.[72] "Oh if I could only send this great tender piece of tenderloin to my friends at home! would not they luxuriate over it? & this enormous heart which lays before me, would I could eat a piece of it boiled under the superintendence of my Mother!" wrote Elisha Perkins.[73]

According to Edwin Bryant, the choicest cuts of a young fat buffalo cow were the rump, tenderloin, liver, heart, tongue, hump, and "an intestinal vessel or organ, commonly called by hunters the 'marrow-gut,' which anatomically speaking, is the chylo-poetic duct. This vessel contains an unctuous matter resembling marrow, and hence its vulgar name. No delicacy which I have ever tasted of the flesh kind can surpass this when properly prepared."[74] Bryant was describing the intestine that mountain cooks used for making sausage.

Buffalo meat, darker and coarser than beef, was either fried in a pan or broiled directly over the hot coals. Bones and tough parts were added to the soup pot. The hump was cut up to eat immediately or made into jerky. One party reported that they buried the large bones in the coals of buffalo chips and in an hour had some delicious baked marrow.[75] Tongues were smoked or pickled. Buffalo tongue became a gourmet food and was shipped to restaurants throughout the country, its popularity contributing to the demise of the buffalo.

Patty Sessions gathered dry weeds to place on the dung before broiling her family's buffalo steaks. Carvalho's companions copied the Indians: "They cut the buffalo meat in strips about an inch thick, four wide, and twelve to fifteen long. The stick is then inserted in the meat, as boys do a kite stick; one end of the stick is then stuck in the ground, near the fire, and the process of roasting is complete—the natural juice of the meat is retained, in this manner, and I think it the most preferable way to cook game."[76] During the meal the men would simply cut a slice off the piece roasting on the stick. Buffalo meat was so versatile that Narcissa Whitman boasted that her husband had a different way of preparing each piece of meat. Unfortunately she did not record the recipes; she did, however, observe that her husband liked the taste of buffalo so much that he now began to do most of the cooking.[77]

Yet there were dissenters. "While here we had buffalo meat. We did not like it very well. It is much coarser than beef," wrote Lucia Williams.[78] Perhaps Williams had been eating meat from an old bull, which Charles Gray implied "tasted like the '*chef d'ouvre*' of the devils kitchen, the most offensive meat I ever tasted & so that I found it impossible to eat it."[79]

Knowing that they must always plan ahead, emigrants preserved the buffalo meat by "jerking" it. In that process the meat is cut into long strips about one inch wide and then dried in the sun or over a fire. The name jerky comes from the Spanish *charqui*, which itself comes from the Peruvian *quichua*. This method of preserving meat has been popular for centuries.

The simplest method for drying meat was to string it on ropes and then hang it on the outside of the wagon cover. There it would soak up the hot sun for two or three days until it was cured; then it was packed in bags and stored for future use. One diarist wrote that the wagons looked as if they were decorated with "coarse red fringe."[80] "The meat was very Black and coarse but we youngsters found it to be good chewing," recalled William Colvig.[81] The "hanging up method," while simple, meant that the meat picked up all the dust and debris from the air. Still, when "hunger stares one in the face one isn't particular about trifles like that," stated Catherine Haun in her detailed diary.[82]

Another way of preparing jerky was to build a scaffold to support the meat over a slow fire and then to smoke the strips. Joel Palmer described the process, which imitated the method used by Native Americans:

> The meat is sliced thin and a scaffold prepared by setting forked sticks in the ground, about three feet high, and laying small poles or sticks crosswise upon them. The meat is laid upon those pieces, as a slow fire built beneath; the heat and smoke completes the process in half a day; and with an occasional sunning the meat will keep for months.[83]

The smoking method required a stopover; but in my twentieth-century view, considering disease and germs, smok-

ing seems safer than air-drying. In any case, however
jerky was prepared, it was popular.

As early as 1844 a few observers deplored the wanton
destruction of the buffalo. The Reverend Edward Parrish
described one buffalo hunt:

> Forty thousand pounds of best beef spoiled in one
> night. The animals were run through the hot sun a
> great part of the day, and then shot down and left to
> lie in the hot sun during the afternoon until near sun-
> set, before they were gutted, and then were left
> through the night with the hide on.[84]

Lorenzo Sawyer asserted that "a wanton destruction of
buffalo, the main dependence of the Indians for food, is
certainly reprehensible," but he added that "the desire of
engaging once at least, in the 'buffalo chase' by the emigrant, can scarcely be repressed."[85] By the time Harriet
Loughary made the trip in 1864 the buffalo herds were on
the way to extinction:

> Some of our men went to day hunting for buffaloe and
> antelope but saw none. While the bleached bones of
> the buffaloe are strewn all along the road, not an ani-
> mal seen. The needless and wanten slaughter of
> these once numerous animals, has almost caused
> them to be extinct.[86]

The issue was also raised in August 1848 in the *American Agriculturist*, a popular magazine of the mid-nineteenth century.

Killing the Buffalo
Notwithstanding the great and wanton destruction of
the buffalo, many years must elapse before the lordly

animal becomes extinct. In spite of their numerous enemies, they will exist in countless numbers, and, could any steps be taken to protect them, as is done in respect to other game, they would ever remain the life and ornament of the boundless prairies.

"A FINE HOTCHPOTCH"

In addition to buffalo meat the emigrants dined on antelope, sage hens, geese, ducks, rabbits, and fish. Commenting on the enormous quantities of fresh meat, Carvalho called one of the cook's creations a "splendid Olla Podrida," a spicy Spanish stew of sausage and other meat, beans, and vegetables. He worried that the bonanza would not last and feared "that we shall want some of things which are now being inconsiderately wasted," a prophetic concern, as the company later became trapped in the mountains during the winter and had to shoot their horses for food.[87]

Antelope meat, which was compared to veal and was considered "much better than venison," customarily received rave reviews. Emigrants indicated that it was juicy, sweet, and tender. "We dined on the leg of an antelope. It sure was a treat," noted Caroline Clark.[88] Her opinion was validated by the responses of several overlanders. When hunters came back with this game, everyone feasted. Lodisa Frizzell depicted the scene at her camp: "Two of our men went out hunting, & succeeded in killing an antelope, & a mountain hare; we soon took their jackets off, & such a broiling, boiling & roasting you never saw."[89]

On one occasion when Francis Sawyer's husband took some extra antelope meat to a neighboring camp, he received a bottle of whiskey; with liquor at two dollars a bottle the Sawyers considered the trade a fine way of saying thanks. Commenting on whiskey's high price, Sawyer explained to her family back home: "That seems like a high price for liquor, but these men have to haul it from the States or from California, over the mountains, across the Great desert and up this river for two hundred miles, so you see it is bound to be a costly drink."[90]

A meal of fish ranked as high as antelope as an outstanding treat; fish were avidly consumed by emigrants lucky enough to catch or to purchase them. "Caught some very fine trout from the Humboldt, and these, with a singular concoction of bacon, hard bread, rice and beans, boiled together, made a fine 'hotchpotch,' which being a change, was well liked. What cooks we are!" exclaimed James Hutchings, the creator of such a savory fish stew.[91] Hutchings, a bachelor, earlier had written: "I wish I had taken lessons in the art of every man his own washerwoman, cook and general housewife." But he obviously had learned his lessons. When the young men traveling with Eleanor Allen caught seven large trout, Allen observed: "Feasted this evening on trout and stewed currants. They were excellent and afforded us a rich repast." The young fishermen had used grasshoppers for bait, "which the fish easily devour."[92] Except for the time that the "mosquitoes were so thick, so brave and resolute," Francis Sawyer's group had fished every day while they were in the vicinity of Soda Springs. On most days they were lucky; other days they "did not get a nibble." Once Sawyer traded "a string of beads to an Indian boy for some fish."[93] Even though Hutchings concocted a fish stew, frying was the usual method of preparing fish. Sizzling, freshly fried fish was always a welcome meal.

As the travelers approached Oregon Territory, they caught or purchased salmon from the Indians. Mary Burrell was thoroughly satisfied with the fish she obtained: "Bought 4 nice Salmon trout of some nearly naked Indians for a loaf of bread & some crackers. We ate the whole 4 for our supper. Splendid." Charles Stevens wrote home that "we got the first taste of Salmon, and you had better think we feasted."[94] Amazingly, salmon was unknown to Harriet Loughary's party, and they declined a purchase "because of its color, believing it to be soiled." The Indians tried to convince them it was good, "but we were as ignorant of their language as of the Salmon."[95]

Sage hen or grouse (*Centrocercus urophasianus*) was not everyone's favorite. Lucena Parsons thought that sage hens were better in September, because "late in the fall they taste of sage." Amelia Hadley emphatically preferred bacon: "see some hens called sage hens, I have heard say that they were good to eat, some of our company killed some, and I think a skunk, prefarable, their meat tastes of this abominable mountain sage." Yet Francis Sawyer "ate them for dinner and thought they were delicious." Charles Gray found them "most decidedly a 'bonne bouche' in these salt pork & bacon times."[96] And when Elisha Perkins had "a real old-fashioned richly seasoned dumpling sage hen soup" with "fine white bread," he said it was the "choicest meal I have eaten on this journey."[97] The soup had been prepared by the captain of an ox train who had invited Perkins for dinner; a week later Perkins ate with another group and was again served a "magnificent sage hen soup." Ducks and geese also turned up in the all-purpose soup pot, sometimes topped with dumplings or mixed with hard bread.

From time to time the elusive prairie dog or the mountain goat ended up on the night's menu. Perkins wrote, "Some [prairie dogs] are so fat that it is necessary to pull off a part before cooking to prevent the meat being too oily." Yet Perkins considered them delicious. Basil Longsworth agreed. The mountain goat did not find such favor, at least from Amelia Hadley: "Had some to eat. I merely tasted it so as to say I had eat some, but do not like it. the rest said it was good but I know they think better all the time for they taste of every thing they get even to black birds and call them good."[98] Amelia's party had traveled twenty-two miles that day, so perhaps she was just too tired to enjoy anything.

AROUND THE CAMPFIRE

Most meal preparations were probably both tedious and difficult. Mary Burrell could not have found cooking enjoyable when she "baked till 12 o'clock at night" or when, several days later, "much lightning and heavy thunder and large hail" caused a "tremendous time getting supper." Nor would Lou Gould, who on a layover day, made herself nearly sick by doing a "large quantity of cooking."[99] And I don't suppose Helen Stewart had a smile on her face when "everybody is in bed but Agnes and myself i believe and we would be there to but we have to wait til the apples are stewed enough."[100] Elizabeth Duncan's comment, "I have been very busy all day baking cooking washing and ironing very tired tonight," echoes entries in many diaries.[101]

Yet in the first months, when supplies were still adequate, many emigrants welcomed mealtimes as a break from the hours spent riding or walking. The aroma from the stewing pot of dried apples and simmering meat and beans surely prompted a sense of camaraderie and encouraged the overlanders to press on and make a new home. "We are in camp to-night . . . among are several ladies. These, like my-

Overland Trail campscene photo (1870). Courtesy of the Oregon
Historical Society (OrHi 5237-A).

self, were engaged in helping to cook supper, and I have no
doubt, but that they all enjoyed it heartily, as I did," reported Frances Sawyer. Earlier, Sawyer had recorded that
"the men do all the cooking in bad weather, though I never
have to do anything but make up the bread."[102] Sarah Sutton observed that the girls in her party "apear very happy.
are all in good health and know no trouble. we have only 8
girls to do all the work this trip is fun for them." Sutton had
recorded that information after spending her day off "washing, and baking aple and peach pies, stewing beans, and ra-
bits." Verifying the joys of mealtimes, Henry Page, anticipating his wife's query about camp life, assured her that
they were managing: "Well I can truly say that I do not mis-
like it, but on the contrary am much pleased with it thus
far—Hank & self have done most of the cooking, and have
succeeded thus far, admirably—the great difficulty we find,
is to cook enough."[103]

Abigail Scott relished the good times, even while dining in a snowstorm:

> Eat breakfast this morning in a snow storm, and altho. the prospect *did* look rather gloomy, still we kept in good cheer, and our victuals, crusted, (not with sugar) but snow, certainly disappeared in a manner that plain showed that we had not lost our appetites even if we were experiencing all the 'delights' of (a) snow storm in the open prairie.

Scott, however, like most of the overlanders, did have good days and bad days. On July 24, 1852, several months after she had written her cheerful letter to her grandfather, she complained about one of the bad days. "The weather is warm, the musquitoes annoying, and a dead animal not far from our [camp] in no way accebarates our enjoyment."[104]

Meals around a campfire and dining outside were a novel experience for most of the travelers. Narcissa Whitman, who made the trip to Oregon Territory in 1837, before the publication of the popular traveler's guides, was the first overlander to offer thoughts on outdoor eating. She was traveling with her husband, Dr. Marcus Whitman, and Eliza and Henry Spalding; the women in this party are considered to have been the first white women to travel the Overland Trail. Narcissa Whitman appreciated campfire cooking and described it to her relatives in the East.

> Tell Mother I am a very good housekeeper in the prairie. I wish she could just take a peep at us while we are sitting at our meals, our table is ground, our table cloth is an India rubber cloth and when it rains . . . a

cloak. . . . Husband always provides my seat and in a
way that you would laugh to see us. . . . We take a
blanket and lay down by the table and those whose
joints will let them follow the fashion, others take out
some of the baggage (I suppose you know that there is
no [stone] in this country) for my part I fix myself as
gracefully as I can some times on a blanket sometimes on a box. . . . let me assure you of this we relish
our food none the less for siting on the ground while
eating.[105]

Other emigrants—both men and women—over a period of years noted the practice of "breaking bread"
around the campfire. One wonders if this act of fellowship
gave the adventurous travelers a feeling of community;
surely it added to the spirit of shared adventure and their
new sense of independence.

Our friends at home would have been amused could
they have looked in on our cooking operations & supper this evening. . . . Our table was a board laid
across two of our camp chests & as we squatted and
knelt round it many were the jokes passed on the nov-
elty and ludicrousness of our situation.[106]

Who would not prefer this to a table profusely covered
with dishes filled with dainties of every kind, shut up
in a house, the work of art! Give me rather fair Nature's beauties shed abroad to my view, and 'twill
lend a charm to everything.[107]

Just imagine 27 of us on our camp ground near the
river bank 3 large covered baggage wagons & 2 car-
riages ranged in a row at a sufficient distance apart

to admit of our tables in their shade 3 of the messes cooking by as many stoves & camp fires. Our suppers are soon ready & our tables which are converted out of our provision boxes are set & 27 of the hungriest folks you ever see are soon set too. some on camp stools & more on the ground ready to fall to at the meal of warm pancakes bacon applesauce & tea with a hearty relish.

Louisa Cook, the author of the last quotation, made the trip twenty-five years after Narcissa Whitman and emphasized the sense of adventure and enthusiasm among the travelers several times in her letters home. Even after several months of travel she thought it "one of the greatest old trips that was ever heard of" and wrote:

You would laugh to see us come into camp about 3 every afternoon tired hungry & of course cross ragged shoes every article of clothing trimed with fringe (all the style here) hoopless spiritless & disposed. . . . but after supper what a change some 6 or 8 camp fires burn brightly round the corell & round these a cheerful group of men & women seated on a box inverted pail or true Indian style squatted on the ground laughing over the exploits of the day.[108]

A food writer observing the cooking that occurred during the journey across the prairies and plains easily could have written about the typical travelers' cuisine replete with foods that would not spoil and dishes that could be prepared by cooks unaccustomed to cooking outdoors. Indeed, if that writer compared the foods used on the Overland Trail with those that might appear in a camper's pack today, more than a few similarities would turn up. Jerky, crackers, dried fruit, bouillon cubes, lemonade mixes, and flour and baking powder mixes for making bread could be found in the emigrant's provision box and in the camper's pack. The overlanders of course had to cook outdoors for four to six months; the typical camper might be in the wilderness for only a few days or at most a couple of weeks. And the camper knows his mixture of flour and baking powder will work; the hardworking emigrant never knew for certain if the flour would be too wet for baking, the crackers a crumbly mix, or the dried fruit soft enough for putting into a piecrust. The emigrant cooks, working under adverse conditions, converted the standard traveler's cuisine into an impressive array of crowd-pleasing meals, and the success of these cooks attests to their culinary ingenuity.

5

THE GLORIOUS FOURTH

"We hoisted a flag belonging to some of the company, and
as we saw the stars and stripes floating in the breeze we
felt quite patriotic."

Colorful firecrackers did not explode over the plains.
Picnic baskets filled with fried chicken, hot dogs, and potato salad did not miraculously appear by the campfire
when the emigrants paid tribute to Independence Day.
But the Fourth of July was celebrated with special foods,
toasts of good cheer, and guns "bursting in air" up and
down the Platte and Sweetwater rivers. On the glorious
Fourth, emigrants "felt quite patriotic."[1]

They were simply joining with the rest of the country
in affirming the spirit of nationalism. The celebration reminded the pioneers of their links to their old homes and
helped them to renew their vows of carrying American
ideas and aspirations to the West. In a show of patriotism
an unidentified correspondent wrote a letter to a St. Joseph newspaper:

Although we occupy an obscure corner in the moral
vineyard, and do not often hear of the ballance of the
world, nor it of us, we know how to celebrate this day
of days to American Citizens and to appreciate the
spilt blood and sleeping ashes of our Fathers.[2]

The idea of a celebration in the midst of such difficult travel is so distinctively American, so much a part of the overlanders outlook, that it is fitting to treat this unique day in detail. How amazing it is that the travelers, weary from at least two months of peregrinations across the continent, still had the energy to throw a party. A close look at the preparations for the celebration and at the ingredients that were stirred and mixed into cakes, puddings, and even ice cream of the Fourth of July completes the picture of the baking, broiling, and eating that took place on the Oregon-California Trail.

AT THE ROCK

Whenever possible, overlanders tried to celebrate the Fourth in the vicinity of Independence Rock in central Wyoming. Supposedly, the rock was named by the early trappers who had first celebrated at that spot, although which trappers and in what year are subjects of much conjecture. Tom Fitzpatrick, Col. William L. Sublette, and the American Fur Company are contenders for the title of who named the rock in either 1824, 1829, or 1830; the answer depends upon which diary account a reader chooses to believe.[3] For the emigrants, inscribing their names on the large monolith became an established ritual.

The grand rock standing so tall and strong was a great curiosity to the emigrants; there was nothing like it at home. Merrill Mattes, in a study of 100 of the best-known journals and guidebooks representing the years 1830–1866, writes that 65 percent of the diarists mentioned Independence Rock.[4] Peter Decker's and Elisha Perkins's descriptions are typical:

Indeed a curiosity in its way 600 yds long & 20 yds wide & some 100 feet high of solid grey granite—

primitive rock rising from the level plain, fine grass & pretty flowers grow at the foot in abundance. Many names inscribed on it of which I saw that of my friend M. N. Wambaugh of California.[5]

Ind. Rock is a huge mass of smooth stone oval, some 1/2 mile long or more rising abruptly out of the plain & standing entirely alone though a little beyond commences the Rocky Mountain range in full view. The greatest attraction & curiosity of Ind. Rock however is the vast number of names inscribed upon it. Being very smooth it makes a fine intelligence board & thousands upon thousands of names are thickly inscribed in large letters on the two sides round which the road winds. . . . Hardly anyone passes without leaving his mark with tar or charcoal.[6]

A YOUNG NATION

In 1851 the country was celebrating the seventy-fifth anniversary of its independence. No doubt a few of the emigrants had grown up with family members who had fought in the War for Independence and who remembered when Congress declared the nation free from Great Britain in 1776. A few of these early citizens might even have recalled that the vote for independence was approved on July 2 but that Congress needed two extra days to debate the wording of the declaration and to formalize the resolution. John Adams had written to his wife, "The second day of July, 1776, will be the most memorable epoch in the history of America. I am apt to believe that it will be celebrated by succeeding generations as the great anniversary Festival."[7] But it was July 4 of course that became the official birthday of the new country.

In his letter to Abigail, John Adams established the guidelines for Fourth of July celebrations:

It ought to be commemorated, as the day of deliverance, by solemn acts of devotion to God Almighty. It ought to be solemnized with pomp and parade, with shows, games, sports, guns, bells, bonfires, and illuminations, from one end of this continent to the other, from this time forward, forevermore.

The first national-holiday celebration took place in Philadelphia on July 8, 1776. The people followed Adams's guidelines and paraded, fired guns, rang bells, and made a bonfire by burning the king's heraldic arms, a painted banner hanging on the state house (they removed the banner before lighting the fire). A year later, on the first anniversary, fireworks were added to the celebration, and the ships in the Philadelphia harbor fired thirteen guns in honor of the colonies. Loud noises, illuminations, thirteen-gun-salutes, and thirteen toasts were common features of the day as the people rejoiced over their new independence.

When John Adams predicted that the holiday would be celebrated with illuminations he was referring to the old-fashioned custom of illuminating buildings and public plazas by placing candles in windows or even atop walls and along public thoroughfares. Fireworks, although a part of the first anniversary celebration, did not become a tradition until the first decade of the nineteenth century. Fireworks were expensive and required advance planning; the war had left the cities poor, and celebrations were unplanned affairs. Yet even though firecrackers were not available, guns were, and exploding shells became a prominent feature of the Fourth. Overlanders continued this tradition.

As on most holidays, an exceptional dinner became

part of the tradition of the Fourth. In the early days, after the men paraded and the guns were fired, the participants marched to a public dinner, prepared by a local tavern-keeper and generally served outside. Only men attended; politics were considered to be of no concern to the women.[8] Ale, cider, wine, rum, or whiskey flowed as everyone toasted the union; drinking too much was accepted.

As the cities grew, one tavernkeeper could no longer prepare all the public dinners, so celebrants hosted private parties. Political parties quickly realized that these events presented a perfect occasion for telling why their candidates should be elected, and political speeches were added to the festivities. The elaborate dinners became picnics, with women and children attending, and the traditions established continue to this day. In a boost for this type of entertainment an editorial in the *St. Louis Missouri Republican*, July 4, 1855, stated:

We confess a liking for the old fashioned style of celebrating the Fourth of July—an oration—a march to a grove—a dinner with sentiments and the etceteras. Fire-works have no particular charm. A mental-treat, even though the subject be considered a hackneyed one, is far better than all the glare and glitter and bluster and noise that can be made.

"THE BEST WE COULD PROVIDE"

Just as family and friends at home varied the dishes in the picnic basket, so did the emigrants. From cornstarch cakes to an elaborate several-course meal, the holiday food depended on the tenacity of the cook and the supplies in the provision box. Even simple food such as the potato could make the meal momentous. "Our dinner, in honor of the national anniversary, was the best we could provide. The last of our potatoes, which had long been saved for the occasion, made it a rare feast," noted Margaret Frink.[9]

Harriet Loughary turned the usual provisions into Fourth of July gastronomic delights by making certain that the beans were baked instead of boiled and only half-cooked and that there would be "some warm bread instead of burned hoe cake." The Loughary party also displayed the flag, shot their guns, and let the children have a picnic; theirs was a typical Fourth of July celebration:

> The few stars and stripes were raised on top of our tents, a line of men drawn up, and a salute fired from a hundred little guns and pistols. Three cheers were lustily given for "Our Country," "The Soldiers in the field" and last though not least "The Captains new Grand baby" . . . All had a "go as you please time" Some hunted or fished, others lounged around camp, while the children had a picnic under the bows of a large pine tree. Two more trains came up today and camp with us greatly enjoying our celebration."

The hoecakes that Loughary did not intend to bake were a quick bread of flour (or often cornmeal) and water that was baked on the greased blade of a hoe set near the fire. *The Kentucky Housewife* gave specific directions for preparing the batter:

SHORT HOE CAKES
Rub two large spoonfuls of butter in a quart of flour till well incorporated, sprinkle in a salt-spoonful of salt, and make it into common biscuit paste or dough with cold sweet milk, knead it well, and roll it out

several times with a roller; then roll it into a sheet a quarter of an inch thick, cut it in oblong cakes, and bake them hastily on a hoe or griddle, having it neatly cleaned and rubbed with butter; turn them over once, and as soon as they are done, split and butter them, and eat them warm.[10]

Emigrant families, particularly those going to Oregon Territory, took hoes along with other farm implements that would be needed for planting gardens in their new homes. In those days of few markets people grew their own fruits and vegetables. For the emigrants who arrived in late autumn, spring-planting time could not come too soon.

Unlike most of the emigrants, Helen Carpenter did not feel that the day was " 'Independence Day' but just the same old jolts with plenty of dust thrown in." Reel, her husband, requested "Corn Starch," however. Carpenter, with her characteristic frankness, responded:

I had never heard of that being a 4th of July dish and further more I did not know to cook it. But he did "Just as Aunt Hannah used to." So I stood by and saw him burn his fingers and scorch the starch which when done was of the consistency of very thin gravy. But we ate it, for on a trip like this one must not be too particular.[11]

Helen Carpenter might not have considered cornstarch a holiday food, but nothing was more appropriate for the Fourth than corn. Native American cuisine included a variety of corn recipes long before that golden grain was introduced to the new European settlers. The popular cornpone comes from an Algonquian word meaning corn cooked as a thin layer of batter on a heated stone.

Reel Carpenter may not have been trying to imitate that dish, but it sounds as if he ended up with the precooked version. If the Carpenters were using real cornstarch, which Helen had included in her list of supplies, the "thin gravy" should have hardened as it cooled. When mixed with water and heated, starch granules burst and form a viscous, jellylike liquid that becomes firm when cooled.[12]

In 1857, the year the Carpenters traveled west, the Glenn Cove Starch Works of Long Island, New York, manufactured a starch product, Maizena, that was suitable for cooking:

> [Maizena is] composed of the flour of the choicest selected white corn, and is the most wholesome, nutritious, and agreeable article of food in the whole range of farinaceous substances; it is not only a choice article of dessert, but in the sick room an excellent substitute for the best Bermuda Arrowroot, being used in the same way.[13]

In 1857, processing starch from corn was a relatively new industry in the United States, introduced in 1841 by an Englishman, Orlando Jones. Prior to this new process, starch was processed from wheat.

Distinctive foods were only a part of William Swain's Fourth of July party. His group honored the day with speeches, songs, and numerous toasts:

> We lay abed late this morn. After a late breakfast, we set about getting fuel for cooking our celebration dinner.
>
> Our celebration of the day was very good, much better than I anticipated. . . . At twelve o'clock we formed a procession and walked under our national

flag to the stand to the tune of "The Star Spangled Banner." The president of the day called the meeting to order. We listened to a prayer by Rev. Mr. Hobart, then remarks and the reading of the Declaration of Independence.

We then marched to the "hall," which was formed by running the wagons in two rows close enough together for the wagon covers to reach from one to the other, thus forming a fine hall roofed by the covers and a comfortable place for the dinner table, which was set down the center.

Dinner consisted of: ham; beans, boiled and baked; biscuits; john cake; apple pie; sweet cake; rice pudding; pickles; vinegar; pepper sauce and mustard; coffee; sugar; and milk. All enjoyed it well.

After dinner the toasting commenced. The boys had raked and scraped together all the brandy they could, and they toasted, hurrayed, and drank till reason was out and brandy was in. I stayed till the five regular toasts were drunk; and then, being disgusted with their conduct, I went to our tent, took my pen, and occupied the remainder of the day in writing to my wife.[14]

The "john cake" or johnnycake that was part of Swain's celebration is another type of flat cake made from corn. The name comes from journeycake and was so named because cornmeal cakes could be easily baked on a hot stone or flat griddle and kept well on journeys. Frequently they were baked like hoecakes, and the names were interchangeable. The first printed recipe for johnnycakes appeared in *American Cookery*, the earliest cookbook written by an American and published in America.

JOHNY CAKE OR HOE CAKE

Scald 1 pint of milk and put to 3 pints of indian meal, and half pint of flower—bake before the fire. Or scald with milk two thirds of the indian meal, or wet two thirds with boiling water, add salt, molasses and shortening, work up with cold water pretty stiff, and bake as above.[15]

"QUITE A NUMBER OF KINDS OF CAKES"

The custom of eating cakes on the Fourth may have started with Capt. John Frémont, the noted explorer and the author of a popular guidebook for the Platte River Road. On July 4, 1842, Frémont's friends in St. Louis provided him with a "large supply of excellent preserves and rich fruit-cake."[16] He thus procured his cake the easy way, but those travelers who followed him baked their own. Frémont's cook did not worry about having the right ingredients. St. Louis was already a busy city—butter, eggs, fruit, and brandy, ingredients for a rich fruit cake, were available. Prairie cooks had to hope their flour was not damp and that the cows were still giving milk.

Lorena Hays's Fourth of July menu contained thirteen different dishes, including "quite a number of kinds of cake";[17] Phoebe Judson baked "cake of three varieties (fruit, pound and sponge)";[18] James Bascom Royal dined on frost cake; William Swain had a choice of johnnycake or sweet cake; and the Conyers feasted on pound cake, fruit cake, jelly cake, Sweetwater cake, and "a dozen or more varieties, both of cake and pies not enumerated."[19] Since no one bothered to include recipes we can only surmise how they were made.

Cakes are made with flour, sugar, a leavening agent,

eggs, butter or shortening, a liquid (usually milk), seasonings, and sometimes fruit. We know that flour, sugar, saleratus (leavening), and seasonings such as cinnamon and
nutmeg were staples that the emigrants started out with
and that the many cows provided milk, cream, and butter.
But where did the emigrants find eggs? Standard pound
and sponge cakes, which several emigrants listed as being
on the menus, require many eggs. By the Fourth of July
most emigrants had traveled past Fort Laramie, and a
large portion would be camped around Independence Rock
in central Wyoming. It is possible that in some years eggs
were for sale at Fort Laramie or from peddlers; if so, cooks
planned ahead and tucked them in with the oats or in the
flour barrel and hoped that they would last. "Then, while
at Omaha father packed a large box of eggs in oats," recalled Susan Walton.[20] Some emigrants started their journey with live chickens, which explains how the Royals
made frost cake: " 'Aunt Chloe' (Shanghai hen) laid an
egg; used as frosting for the cake."[21] Perhaps the cook followed the recipe from *Mrs. Hale's New Cook Book*:

ICING FOR CAKE

Beat the white of 1 egg perfectly light—then add 8
teaspoonsful of loaf sugar, pounded fine and sifted,
very gradually, beating it well; after every spoonful,
add one drop of the essence of lemon or rose-water to
flavor it.[22]

Though desirable, eggs are not necessary for all kinds
of cakes, and in the nineteenth century it was not unusual
to make cakes without eggs. Hens did not lay eggs during
the short winter days; there was not enough light or
warmth in the henhouse to raise their young. Only those
cooks who took care to protect stored eggs had fresh ones in

the wintertime. Nineteenth-century cookbook authors routinely offered recipes for cakes without eggs.

An eggless cake recipe belonging to Alice Grierson, the wife of a frontier soldier, is probably typical of the cake the emigrants ate on the glorious Fourth. Grierson's collection of 600 recipes included several cakes without eggs; to distinguish the recipes she gave them numbers.

CAKE WITHOUT EGGS—NO. 1
2 cups and a half of flour, one cup of sugar, one cup sweet milk, one half cup of butter, one teaspoonful of cream of tartar, one half of soda. Flavor with lemon.[23]

Other eggless cake recipes found in early cookbooks provide examples of the kinds of cakes the emigrants must have baked on that special day.

GINGER BREAD
1/2 cup of sugar, 1/2 cup of molasses, 1/4 cup of butter, 1/4 cup of lard, 2 cups of flour, 1 tablespoon of ginger, 1/2 teaspoon of soda [saleratus]; dissolve soda in 1/2 cup of boiling water; a pinch of salt.[24]

FRUIT CAKE WITHOUT EGGS
1 pound fat pork chopped fine; pour over it 1 pint boiling water or coffee, 2 cups molasses, 1 cup sugar, 2 pounds raisins, 1 pound currants, 2 tablespoons cinnamon, 1 tablespoon nutmeg, 1 tablespoon allspice, 1 teaspoon soda, 8 cups flour.

The pound and sponge cakes that Phoebe Judson and E. W. Conyers baked would have presented the most trouble because these cakes traditionally call for at least ten to twelve eggs. The cakes may not have been true sponge or pound cakes, but those travelers who wrote about them thought the cakes tasted as good as the real thing. Perhaps the emigrants thought a fancier name made the cakes sound better. Moreover, the comments about pound and sponge cakes come from journals written after the journey. In the same tradition as the caught fish that kept on getting bigger, the plain eggless cake kept growing lighter. Nevertheless, the emigrant cooks outdid themselves in baking cakes to serve at the Fourth of July dinners.

ICE CREAM AT THE SOUTH PASS

Ice cream desserts were also featured at several of the holiday celebrations. Taking advantage of the snow in the mountains, ingenious cooks sweetened milk, packed it into containers, and froze the concoction in makeshift ice cream machines. Thanks to Charles Parke, an explicit recipe survives:

After crossing Sweetwater for the last time, we traveled up the valley 10 miles and camped on a small brook, arriving at 1:00 P.M., where we laid over all afternoon. This being the nation's birthday and our under clothing not as clean as we could wish, we commenced our celebration by "washing dirty linen" or rather woolens, as we all wore woolen shirts. Washing done and shirts hung out to dry—we never iron—all hands set about enjoying themselves as best they could. Some visited two large banks of snow about half a mile from the ford on Sweetwater. Having plenty of milk from two cows we had with us, I determined to [do] something no other living man ever did in this place and on this sacred day of the year, and that was to make *Ice Cream at the South Pass of the Rockies.*

I procured a small tin bucket which held about 2 quarts. This I sweetened and flavored with *peppermint*—had nothing else. This bucket was placed inside a wooden bucket, or Yankee Pale, and the top put on. Nature had supplied a huge bank of coarse snow, or hail, nearby, which was just the thing for this *new factory.* With alternate layers of this, and salt between the two buckets and aid of a *clean* stick to stir with, I soon produced the most delicious ice cream tasted in this place. In fact, the whole company so decided, and as a compliment drew up in front of our Tent and fired a Salute, bursting one gun but injuring no one.[25]

The Conyers party also feasted on ice cream. Sent out to hunt game for the Fourth of July dinner, the hunters found a huge snowball, which they carried back to camp by inserting a pole through the center. "The snowball was brought into use in making a fine lot of Sweetwater Mountain ice cream," noted E. W. Conyers.[26] Presumably the cooks used a variation of Parke's method since his recipe was similar to those found in period cookbooks. Besides providing instructions for making the ice cream, early culinary experts furnished recipes for various ice cream flavors such as vanilla, chocolate, strawberry, peach, sassafras, gooseberry, and quince.

Ice cream was known in America in the early eighteenth century. George Washington was an ice cream lover, and Dolly Madison served ice cream to add distinction to her White House dinner parties. But it was not until 1846 that an American, Nancy Johnson, invented a special machine for making ice cream. Her portable hand-cranked churn beat the mixture of cream and flavoring with a dasher (paddle) as the mixture froze. The invention revolutionized ice cream production because it resulted in a smoother-tasting ice cream, enabling anyone who had the machine to make the best quality of ice cream at home.

Like other emigrants, the Conyers spent a remarkable Fourth and ushered in the day with the firing of guns and the singing of "The Star-Spangled Banner." The preparations began on July 3 when a "number of wagon beds are taken to pieces and formed into long tables." Everyone was involved. The men gathered wood and hunted for game, and the women made a flag and prepared a sumptuous repast. The momentous day featured a fantastic feast:

> The day was ushered in with the booming of small arms, which was the best that we could do under the circumstances, so far away from civilization. Although the noise was not so great as that made by cannon, yet it answered the purpose. Just before the sun made its appearance above the eastern horizon, we raised our forty-foot flagstaff with "Old Glory" nailed fast to the top, which waved as majestically and graceful as though it had been made of the best Japan silk. After the flagstaff was raised to its position our company circled around the old flag and sung "The Star Spangled Banner." Then three rousing cheers and a tiger were given to "Old Glory.". . . All gathered around the tables loaded with refreshments, beautified and decorated with evergreens and wild flower of the valley, that speak volumes in behalf of the good taste displayed by the ladies, both in the decorative and culinary art. The following is our bill of fare in part:

MEATS

Roast Antelope, Roast Sagehen, Roast Rabbit, Antelope Stew, Sagehen Stew, Jack-Rabbit Stew, Antelope Potpie, Sagehen Fried, Jack Rabbit Fried.

VEGETABLES

Irish Potatoes (brought from Illinois), Boston Baked Beans, Rice, Pickles.

BREAD

White Bread, Graham Bread, Warm Rolls, fresh from the oven.

PASTRY

Pound Cake, Fruit Cake, Jelly Cake, Sweetwater Mountain Cake, Peach Pie, Apple Pie, Strawberry Pie, Custard Pie. (A dozen or more varieties, both of cake and pies not enumerated.)

DRINKS

Coffee, Tea, Chocolate, and Good, Cold Mountain Water, fresh from the brook. . . .

No person left the table hungry. After our feast patriotic songs were indulged in, winding up with three cheers for Uncle Sam and three for Old Glory. Of course, the ladies were not forgotten, and three rousing cheers were given for them. Take it altogether, we passed an enjoyable day—a Fourth of July on the plains never to be forgotten.[27]

"OTHER LITTLE DISHES"

On the Fourth, emigrants made a special attempt to obtain fresh meat. Soups, stews, and fried or roasted victuals prepared from antelopes, sage hens, buffalo, fish, and wild fowl were featured attractions at holiday tables. The Buckinghams "breakfasted at six upon Trout Strawberries & cream."[28] Francis Sawyer's family "went fishing this morning, then came back and cooked a good dinner." Chester Ingersoll killed a buffalo and served it for dinner, and Harry Rudd killed an antelope. Since his wife Lydia had recently made fresh gooseberry sauce, perhaps they used it as a sauce for the fresh-cooked game. An old recipe shows that gooseberry sauce was easy to prepare.

GOOSEBERRY SAUCE

Gather gooseberries when ripe, take off the stems and blossom ends, pour boiling water on them, and stew them in a covered pan till done and the liquor low: then add half a pound of sugar to each pound of berries, and a small lump of butter, rolled in flour; stew them a few minutes longer and serve them. They are a nice concomitant to roasted poultry and game.[29]

The cook accompanying the Scottish lord Sir William Drummond Stewart outdid himself on the glorious Fourth. According to Matthew Field, a reporter traveling with Sir William, the cook prepared "Gumbo, *boudon*, tongue, forced meat balls."[30] Sir William, a rich Scotsman making his second trip to the West, was going only as far as the Rocky Mountains. Thirty-five other gentlemen made the trip, an adventurous hunting expedition in the mountains. Field, later writing about that day for his paper, the *New Orleans Daily Picayune*, elaborated on the Fourth of July meal (Field regularly sent back amusing reports of the "boys day out" in the wilderness):

Sketch

Two of the largest tents in camp were stretched in connection, giving a large space for the guests, who made themselves comfortable in cross-legged fashion, firmly deposited upon *terra firma*, along the sides of a long strip of oil-cloth laid out upon the grass. The viands displayed upon the oil-cloth were buffalo hump ribs, buffalo side ribs, buffalo tongues, buffalo marrow bones, buffalo "sweetbreads," and buffalo *et ceteras*. Most excellent plum pudding was manufactured by an amateur *cuisinier*, and juleps of legitimate mixture were among the luxuries of the feast.

Martha Read's group had just reached buffalo country when she recorded, "Had some buffalo meat for the first time. Found it very good eating. We feel thankful that we are spared to celebrate another American Independence Day here in these lonesome wilds where there is so much sickness and death."[31] And Samuel Dundass, "despairing of a patriotic manifestation with our own train, resolved to join our Illinois friends in their celebration—sharing in the sequel of their performances an excellent dish of wild ducks."[32] Exceptional and plentiful food was a rousing success as the emigrants saluted Old Glory.

Around several campfires the meat was baked in savory pies. "The crowning piece of the feast was a savory pie, made of sage hen and rabbit, with a rich gravy; the crust having been raised with yeast, was as light as a feather," recalled Phoebe Judson. Before being placed into the pie dough, the meat was fried, stewed, or roasted; the juices and fat rendered provided the gravy. Judson does not tell us the spices or vegetables she used, but one can imagine that she at least had some wild onions, salt, and pepper. Reminiscing about that Fourth of July fifty years later, Judson wrote, "Not one of them is so vividly portrayed upon my mind as the one celebrated by the little band of adventurers, so far from civilization."[33]

Any food that was not used every day became noteworthy on the Fourth, and canned foods came under that category. Along with freshly caught fish, the Sawyers had "canned vegetables, . . . rice cakes and other little dishes."[34] Randall Hewitt perked up the soup and stew pots with canned tomatoes. In 1862 that was such a rare treat that he expounded on the merits of having them on the Fourth of July:

> A fitting close of our patriotic demonstrations of the day was in having an addition to our bill of fare at supper, which almost raised that uniform meal to the dignity of a banquet. Among our commissary stores were two or three cans of tomatoes which had kept remarkably well; they had been carefully preserved for some signal event, no doubt; and here was the event. To further signalize the "day we celebrate," two cans were opened, and their contents served in stew and soup. The company thought nothing ever tasted half so good. Taking surroundings into account with steady service of bacon and beans this simple vegetable came very near being the delightful change it was said to be, on that patriotic occasion. Perhaps it was the only time tomatoes were ever served as a course at a Fourth of July banquet.[35]

Hewitt made a good assumption; tomato-based entrees were not popular Fourth of July dishes. But at least one other family, the Royals, served "preserved tomatoes" at their celebration dinner. The Hewitts and the Royals were following the established custom of serving only cooked tomatoes; in that era, raw tomatoes were thought to be unhealthy. Eliza Leslie's popular book, *Directions for Cookery*, advised in 1848 that tomatoes "will not lose their raw taste in less than three hours cooking"; and in 1860, *Godey's Lady's Book*, the bible of the American housewife, repeated that advice.[36]

Hewitt's canned tomatoes may have had a second distinction. Like corn, tomatoes are a new-world food, having originated in Peru. Joseph Campbell, of Campbell soup fame, had entered the canning business in the 1860s and by 1869, along with Abram Anderson, had established a canning firm that specialized in choice vegetables, including "beefsteak tomatoes."[37] Could Hewitt's tomatoes have been the forerunner of Campbell's tomato soup?

The award for the most elaborate dinner surely goes to the women in the Conyers group, but the two women who baked desserts for the Washington City and California Mining Company deserve the distinction of being the most overworked. They had mixed dough, rolled crusts, and stewed fruit to make pies and puddings for ninety-two men. The event was so impressive that it is mentioned in at least two diaries, Henry Austin's and Capt. J. Goldsborough Bruff's. Austin was a doctor with the company and Bruff its leader.

But in spite of wind or weather the cooks of the day commenced their culinary operations—The two ladies, Mrs. Thomas and Miss —— prepared the desert which consisted of peach and apple pies and pudding, rice pudding, stewed apple and peaches.

The ladies honored us with their presence on the occasion; and to them we were indebted for several pounds of dried apples, and decent pastry.[38]

Not everyone of course dined on decent pastry or ate savory pies. George Keller had to make do with "a Fourth of July dinner on musty hard bread, and beef bones in a state of *incipient putrefaction*" that he said was "highly relished by us, as any of the more *sumptuous* repasts served up to our friends in the states."[39] Amos Steck was less appreciative of his humble fare. He recorded in disgust that after having "no other refreshment than hard Bread for dinner, and poor bread at that, [he] will feel little patriotic ardor stimulating him even on this Great Day."[40] Steck had spent the day "driving a slow ox team in a sandy road, his eyes filled & his throat choked with it." Some diarists ignored the day and presumably dined on ordinary fare.

A LITTLE TOO MUCH FIREWATER

"Of course, it was a matter of mathematical certainty that some of us would get 'glorious' upon the 'Glorious Fourth,' and most gloriously were all such patriotic resolutions carried out," wrote Matthew Field to his paper, the *New Orleans Daily Picayune*.[41] For large numbers of weary travelers, no Fourth of July was complete without copious toasts and the appropriate beverages.

Drinking was not confined to holidays, but on the Fourth one did not need the excuse of ill health to imbibe. Many emigrants took advantage of the national celebration and joined in the toasts and merrymaking. "This being the 4th of July the men must needs show their 'independence'; and such another drunken, crazy, hooting, quarreling fighting frolic I seldom witnessed," wrote Jason Lee, a missionary.[42] Drinking was enjoyed by quite a few men in celebrations along the Platte River Road.

Charles Stanton, in a letter to his brother, acknowledged that

> yesterday, as I said before, we celebrated the 4th of July. The breaking one or two bottles of good liquor, which had been hid to prevent a few old tapsters from stealing, (so thirsty do they become on this route for liquor of any kind, that the stealing of it is thought no crime), . . . song and toast, created one of the most pleasurable excitements we have had on the road."[43]

E. W. Conyers made no excuses for too much "firewater" when he described how the men had to prop up their chosen speaker. Either the alcohol had no effect on his oratorical skills or else everyone had had too much to care:

> The question came up, To whom should the honor be given to deliver the oration? This honor fell to the lot of Virgil J. N. Ralston. . . . Unfortunately he with several other young men of our company, went this morning to the Devil's Gate, where they obtained a little too much "firewater," and by the time they reached the camp were considerably under its influence. But this was the glorious old Fourth, therefore the oration we must have. The Declaration of Independence was read by R. L. Doyle, of Keokuk, Ia., after which several of the boys gathered around Virgil, lifting him bodily upon the end of one of our long tables, where they steadied him until he became sufficiently braced up, and then let go of him. He spoke for over half an hour, and delivered, off-hand, an excellent oration.[44]

Not everyone, of course, got drunk; and some emigrants just drank a toast. Virginia Reed, a thirteen-year-old girl who was one of the survivors of the Donner party, wrote about the Fourth:

> We selabrated the 4 of July on plat [Platte River] at Bever criek several of the Gentemen in Springfield gave paw a botel of licker and said it shoulden be opend till the 4 day of July and paw was to look to the east and drink it and they was to look to the West an drink it at 12 o'clock paw treted the company and we all had some lemminade, maw and paw is well.[45]

As they settled into their new homes, the pioneers kept the spirit of the glorious Fourth. The holiday remained a celebration of patriotism and a connection to those families and friends back home. Thus, even for the emigrants and just as John Adams predicted, with noise and dressing up, the display of the flag, and brilliant and boring orations, the Fourth of July was and still is "celebrated by succeeding generations as the great anniversary Festival."

EPILOGUE

The vigorous boiling of the cookery crock slowed to a simmer as the emigrants made the final push over the mountains to their new homes. After leaving Fort Hall, strate-
gically located just before the California and Oregon
routes diverged, emigrants had to make do with short supplies and shorter tempers. After four to six months of travel they were tired; every cookery hint learned and every
scrap of food received took on added importance as cooks
struggled to put food on the table. "Rations grew shorter
and shorter. A real relish was prepared for one meal by
boiling an antiquated ham bone and adding to the liquid,
in which it was boiled, the few scrapings from the dough
pan in which the biscuit from our last measure of flour—
which, by the way, was both musty and sour—had been
mixed," Leslie Scott recalled, describing her family's
hardships as they crossed the Cascade Mountains on their
way to Oregon.[1]

Many travelers would not have made it to the fertile
farmland of Oregon or the goldfields of California if the
established residents of those states had not sent out relief parties to offer food to the exhausted travelers. Eighteen fifty-two was a particularly bad year for travel, as
Martha Read noted in a letter written after she had settled in Oregon:

I wished myself back but I feel thankful that our lives were spared. it was distressing to see how many widows and widowers and orphans were left on the road and a great many would have suffered for want of provisions if the people from Oregon had not gone out with provisions to meet the emigrants. those that were not able to buy, they gave it to them.

Once the emigrants reached their destination, their troubles were not over—particularly in the parts of Oregon Territory that were mostly wilderness. Although merchants arrived along with the large influx of emigrants, stores in the new territories were not well stocked as supplies had to be sent by boat from California or hauled in on packhorses. The situation was somewhat better in California, which had been settled earlier and had more commercial establishments; it was also closer to the supply routes. Still, unless an emigrant claimed land near the more populated areas, obtaining basic food supplies remained a problem. Making it through the first winter was one more hazard for the weary emigrants. "I ate enough rabbit then to last me the rest of my life. . . . Breakfast, dinner and supper the year around scarcely varied those first few years," recalled an early pioneer.[2]

While women in the East attended cooking schools and learned to make "dainty" salads and "refined" cabbage, some of the pioneer women who had struggled across half the continent still cooked on open fires, baked their own bread, hunted and fished for meat, and wrestled roosters for corn seed:

She had just a half cupful of seed corn which she had brought with her. This was very precious as nowhere could any be obtained out here. While she was digging the ground her old rooster sneaked up behind her and gobbled up the corn. When she saw what had happened, without any hesitation, she killed the rooster, recovered the corn from his crop and planted her garden.[3]

Though finding water and fuel was no longer a problem, the emigrants faced a range of other difficulties in their new homes. Their situation of course depended on the year they arrived and on who had come before them. If the previous summer had yielded a good crop so that extras such as potatoes were for sale, if the winter was mild and the cattle survived, if the spring was dry enough to plant an early garden, then the first year was considered easy. But if the rains fell all spring and planting was delayed, if supplies ran short and prices rose, or if sickness struck, then it was hard times for the emigrants.

Generally, the cookery skills the emigrants had learned on the Overland Trail served them well as they settled into their new surroundings. The diaries from the early settlement period in Oregon Territory emphasize that the ability to adapt and to substitute in the kitchen contributed to making a successful home. Tales of making marmalade out of carrots, using cooked green tomatoes as a flavoring for stews and as an ingredient for mincemeat pie, and making pumpkin pie with beans and calling it a delicacy illustrate that the ingenuity carried in the provision box was unpacked and put to use in the new kitchen. Taking pride in providing meals on the trail was surely carried over to taking pride in establishing a new home. In meeting the challenges of trail cooking—what to eat and how to prepare it—the emigrants revealed their strength and spirit. In few circumstances have Americans been as inventive as the cooks on the Oregon-California Trail. Their ingenuity and courage deserve our belated salute.

NOTES

CHAPTER 1. STOCKING UP

1. Lillian Schlissel, *Women's Diaries of the Westward Journey* (New York: Schocken Books, 1982), p. 167.

2. Kenneth L. Holmes, ed., *Covered Wagon Women: Diaries and Letters from the Western Trails*, 10 vols. to date (Glendale, Calif.: Arthur H. Clark Company, 1983–), 5:37.

3. Phoebe Goodell Judson, *A Pioneer's Search for an Ideal Home* (Bellingham, Wash.: printed by Union Printing, Binding, and Stationary Company, 1925), p. 56.

4. John D. Unruh, *The Plains Across* (Urbana: University of Illinois Press, 1979). See chapters 1 and 2 for a discussion of people for and against the westward movement.

5. Joel Palmer, *Journal of Travels over the Rocky Mountains* (Cleveland, Ohio: Arthur Clark Company, 1906), p. 260.

6. Dale L. Morgan, ed., *Overland in 1846*, 2 vols. (Georgetown, Calif.: Talisman Press, 1963), 2:483–84.

7. Ibid., p. 608.

8. *St. Joseph Gazette*, July 30, 1851.

9. Don Ofe, site supervisor, Neligh Mills Historic Site, Nebraska, correspondence, February 28, 1992.

10. *A Country Kitchen* (Maynard, Mass.: Chandler Press, 1987); reprinted from Mary Cornelius, *The Young Housekeeper's Friend* (1850).

11. Holmes, ed., *Covered Wagon Women*, 2:278.

12. Peter H. Burnett, "Letters of Peter H. Burnett," *Oregon Historical Society Quarterly* 3 (1902): 419.

13. Mary Rockwood Powers, *A Woman's Overland Journal to California* (Fairfield, Wash.: Ye Galleon Press, 1985), p. 23.

14. Charles Howard Crawford, *Scenes of Earlier Days* (Chicago: Quadrangle Books, 1898), p. 3.

15. Holmes, ed., *Covered Wagon Women*, 4:244-45.

16. Material on saleratus is from William Woys Weaver, *America Eats* (New York: Harper and Row, 1989), pp. 133-35, and Audrey Ensminger and M. E. Ensminger, *Foods and Nutrition Encyclopedia*, vol. 1 (Clovis, Calif.: Pegus Press, 1983), p. 151.

17. Catherine E. Beecher, *Miss Beecher's Domestic Receipt Book* (New York: Harper and Brothers, 1856), p. 130.

18. Palmer, *Journal of Travels over the Rocky Mountains*, p. 79.

19. Lodisa Frizzell, *Across the Plains to California in 1852* (New York: New York Public Library, 1915), p. 28; edited from original manuscript.

20. Holmes, ed., *Covered Wagon Women*, 3:77, 1:126, 1:180.

21. Merrill J. Mattes, "The Sutler's Store at Fort Laramie," *Annals of Wyoming* (1946), 18:99.

22. James O'Barr, museum curator, De Soto National Wildlife Refuge, Missouri Valley, Iowa, correspondence, February 26, 1992. For more information about the *Bertrand* see Jerome Petsche, *The Steamboat Bertrand* (Missouri Valley, Iowa: Midwest Interpretive Association, 1974).

23. Mattes, "Sutler's Store," p. 99.

24. Eliza Leslie, *Directions for Cookery* (Philadelphia: Henry C. Baird, 1857), p. 435.

25. *Told by the Pioneers*, vol. 2 (Olympia, Wash.: Works Project Administration, 1937), p. 72.

26. S. H. Taylor, "Oregon Bound 1853," *Oregon Historical Society Quarterly* 22 (1921): 141.

27. Holmes, ed., *Covered Wagon Women*, 8:64.

28. Sarah J. Hale, *Mrs. Hale's New Cookbook* (Philadelphia: T. B. Peterson and Brothers, 1857), p. 430.

29. Burnett, "Letters," p. 419.

30. Taylor, "Oregon Bound 1853," p. 141.

31. Randolph B. Marcy, *The Prairie Traveler: A Handbook for Overland Expeditions* (New York: Harper and Brothers, 1859), p. 34.

32. Richard M. Dorson, ed., *Folklore and Folklife* (Chicago: University of Chicago Press, 1972), p. 329.

33. Morgan, ed., *Overland in 1846*, 2:524.

34. Lettice Bryan, *The Kentucky Housewife*, (1839; reprint, Columbia: University of South Carolina Press, 1991), p. 316.

35. *Western Journal* 1 (1848): 228.

36. Albert S. Bolles, *Industrial History of the United States* (Norwich, Conn.: Henry Bill Publishing Company, 1881), p. 81.

37. William Woys Weaver, *Sauerkraut Yankees* (Philadelphia: University of Pennsylvania Press, 1983), pp. 154–55.

38. Marcia Byrom Hartwell, *A Sampler of Recipes 1796 to 1908* (Northampton, Mass.: privately printed, 1984), p. 18.

39. Peter Decker, *The Diaries of Peter Decker: Overland to California in 1849* (Georgetown, Calif.: Talisman Press, 1966), p. 158.

40. Richard Osborn Cummings, *The American and His Food* (Chicago: University of Chicago Press, 1940), p. 111.

41. Leslie, *Directions for Cookery*, p. 336.

42. Cummings, *American and His Food*, p. 111.

43. Bernard J. Reid, *Overland to California with the Pioneer Line* (Stanford, Calif.: Stanford University Press, 1983), p. 97.

44. Holmes, ed., *Covered Wagon Women*, 5:154.

45. Morgan, ed., *Overland in 1846*, 2:540.

46. Sandra L. Myres, ed., *Ho for California! Women's Overland Diaries from the Huntington Library* (San Marino, Calif.: Huntington Library, 1980), p. 147.

47. Holmes, ed., *Covered Wagon Women*, 8:69.

48. Marcy, *Prairie Traveler*, p. 30.

49. Alonzo Delano, *Life on the Plains and among the Diggings* (Auburn, N. Y.: Miller, Orton, and Mulligan, 1854), p. 27.

50. Hale, *Mrs. Hale's New Cookbook*, p. 203.

51. Joseph R. Conlin, *Bacon, Beans, and Galantines* (Reno: University of Nevada Press, 1986), p. 14.

52. Charles Gray, *The Overland Journal of Charles Glass Gray* (San Marino, Calif.: Huntington Library, 1976), p. 14.

53. Bert Webber, ed., *The Oregon and California Trail Diary of Jane Gould in 1862* (Medford, Oreg.: Webb Research Group, 1987), p. 16.

54. David De Wolf, "Diary of the Overland Trail, 1849, and Letters, 1849–1850 of Captain David De Wolf," *Transactions of the Illinois State Historical Society* (Springfield: Illinois State Historical Society, 1926), p. 191.

55. Holmes, ed., *Covered Wagon Women*, 9:72, 5:269.

56. Decker, *Diaries*, p. 147.

57. Gray, *Overland Journal*, p. 5.

58. Schlissel, *Women's Diaries of the Westward Journey*, p. 173.

59. J. S. Holliday, "On the Gold Rush Trail," *American West* 5:4 (July 1968): 38.

60. Myres, ed., *Ho for California*, p. 147.

61. Sandra Myres, *Westering Women and the Frontier Experience* (Albuquerque: University of New Mexico Press, 1982), p. 123.

62. Holmes, ed., *Covered Wagon Women*, 6:252.

63. R. Douglas Hurt, *Indian Agriculture in America* (Lawrence: University Press of Kansas, 1987), p. 29.

64. Charlotte Stearns Pengra, *Diary of Mrs. Bynon J. Pengra* (1853; reprint, Eugene, Oreg.: Lane County Pioneer Historical Society, 1959), p. 24.

65. Holmes, ed., *Covered Wagon Women*, 1:237, 4:244.

66. Myres, ed., *Ho for California*, p. 173.

67. Taylor, "Oregon Bound in 1853," p. 141.

68. Decker, *Diaries*, p. 67.

69. Holmes, ed., *Covered Wagon Women*, 2:75.

70. Georgiana Hill, *How to Cook Potatoes, Apples, Eggs, and Fish Four Hundred Different Ways* (New York: Dick and Fitzgerald, 1869), p. 240.

71. Reubin Gold Thwaites, ed., *Original Journals of the Lewis and Clark Expedition, 1804–1806*, vol. 3 (New York: Dodd, Mead and Company, 1904), p. 71.

72. John B. Wyeth, *Oregon* (Ann Arbor, Mich.: University Microfilms, 1966), p. 30.

73. Taylor, "Oregon Bound 1853," p. 148.

74. Solomon N. Carvalho, *Incidents of Travel and Adventure in the Far West* (Philadelphia: Jewish Publications Society of America, 1954), p. 198. Carvalho cannot be considered a typical emigrant, but I have included his comments about food because he used some of the "new foods" that were being developed.

75. Burnett, "Letters," p. 419.

76. Holmes, ed., *Covered Wagon Women*, 1:44, 5:134n56, 8:63–64.

77. Sam'l P. Arnold, *Eating Up the Santa Fe Trail* (Niwot: University Press of Colorado, 1990), p. 21.

78. John Hull Brown, *Early American Beverages* (Rutland, Vt.: Charles E. Tuttle Company, 1966), p. 78.

79. Merrill J. Mattes, *The Great Platte River Road* (1969; reprint, Lincoln: University of Nebraska Press, 1987), p. 50.

80. Holmes, ed., *Covered Wagon Women*, 8:64.

81. Gray, *Overland Journal*, p. 25.

82. E. W. Conyers, "Diary of E. W. Conyers," *Transactions, Oregon Pioneer Association*, 33d annual reunion (Portland, 1905), p. 425.

83. Holmes, ed., *Covered Wagon Women*, 4:54.

84. Basil N. Longsworth, *The Diary of Basil N. Longsworth* (Portland, Oreg.: Historical Records Survey, 1938), p. 14 (transcription).

85. Myres, ed., *Ho for California*, p. 93.

86. Holmes, ed., *Covered Wagon Women*, 3:258; 4:244; 1:119, 215.

87. De Wolf, "Diary and Letters," p. 191.

88. Bolles, *Industrial History of the United States*, p. 132, 127-34.

89. *Country Kitchen*, N.p.

90. Myres, ed., *Ho for California*, p. 105.

CHAPTER 2. THE MOBILE PANTRY

1. Kenneth L. Holmes, ed., *Covered Wagon Women: Diaries and Letters from the Western Trails*, 10 vols. to date (Glendale, Calif.: Arthur H. Clark Company, 1983–), 5:84.

2. James Hutchings, *Seeking the Elephant, 1849, James M. Hutchings' Overland Journal* (Glendale, Calif.: Arthur H. Clark Company, 1980), pp. 97–98.

3. S. H. Taylor, "Oregon Bound 1853," *Oregon Historical Society Quarterly* 22 (1921): 140.

4. Dale L. Morgan, ed., *Overland in 1846*, 2 vols. (Georgetown, Calif.: Talisman Press, 1963), 2:565.

5. Peter H. Burnett, "Letters of Peter H. Burnett," *Oregon Historical Society Quarterly* 3 (1902): 417.

6. Holmes, ed., *Covered Wagon Women*, 1:32.

7. Velma A. Williams, "Diary of a Trip across the Plains in 1853," *Transactions, Oregon Pioneer Association*, 47th annual reunion (Portland, 1919), p. 179.

8. For detailed information about the construction of covered wagons, see Michael A. Capps, "Wheels in the West: The Overland Wagon," *Overland Journal* 8:4 (1990): 2–11.

9. Chester Ingersoll, *Overland to California in 1847* (Fairfield, Wash.: Ye Galleon Press, 1970), p. 13.

10. Susan Walton, *Wagon Days with Mother Walton* (1931; manuscript, University of Washington Special Collections, Seattle), p. 6.

11. Holmes, ed., *Covered Wagon Women*, 5:28–29, 3:19.

12. Charlotte Stearns Pengra, *Diary of Mrs. Bynon J. Pengra* (1853; reprint, Eugene, Oreg.: Lane County Pioneer Historical Society, 1959), p. 4.

13. Elisha Perkins, *Gold Rush Diary: Being the Journal of Elisha Douglass Perkins on the Overland Trail in the Spring and Summer of 1849* (Lexington: University of Kentucky Press, 1967), p. 5.

14. Violet Coe Mumford and the Royal Family Association, *The Royal Way West*, 2 vols. (Baltimore: Gateway Press, 1988), 2:26.

15. Virginia Wilcox Ivins, *Pen Pictures of Early Western Days* (n.p., 1905), pp. 54–55.

16. Mumford, *Royal Way West*, 2:21.

17. Sandra L. Myres, ed., *Ho for California! Women's Overland Diaries from the Huntington Library* (San Marino, Calif.: Huntington Library, 1980), p. 114.

18. Holmes, ed., *Covered Wagon Women*, 1:216–17.

19. Phoebe Goodell Judson, *A Pioneer's Search for An Ideal Home* (Bellingham, Wash.: Union Printing, Binding, and Stationary Company, 1925), p. 14.

20. Holmes, ed., *Covered Wagon Women*, 6:69.

21. Ibid., 1:214, 5:149.

22. Decker, *Diaries*, p. 63.

23. Jeanne Watson, ed., *To the Land of Gold and Wickedness: The 1848–59 Diary of Lorena L. Hays* (St. Louis: Patrice Press, 1988), p. 37.

24. Ingersoll, *Overland to California in 1847*, p. 13.

25. Decker, *Diaries*, p. 63.

26. Dale L. Morgan, ed., *The Overland Diary of James A. Pritchard* (Denver: Old West Publishing Company, 1959), p. 123.

27. Holmes, ed., *Covered Wagon Women*, 5:28.

28. Edwin Bryant, *What I Saw in California* (New York: D. Appleton and Company, 1848), p. 21.

29. Holmes, ed., *Covered Wagon Women*, 4:287.

30. Myres, ed., *Ho for California*, p. 129.

31. Perkins, *Gold Rush Diary*, pp. 45–46.

32. Hutchings, *Seeking the Elephant*, p. 97.

33. Solomon N. Carvalho, *Incidents of Travel and Adventure in the Far West* (Philadelphia: Jewish Publications Society of America, 1954), p. 85.

34. Holmes, ed., *Covered Wagon Women*, 5:27.

35. Morgan, *Overland in 1846*, 2:530, 565, 515.

36. Holmes, ed., *Covered Wagon Women*, 5:149.

37. Lodisa Frizzell, *Across the Plains to California in 1852* (New York: New York Public Library, 1915), p. 12; edited from original manuscript.

38. Ingersoll, *Overland to California in 1847*, p. 14.

39. Holmes, ed., *Covered Wagon Women*, 1:216.

40. *St. Louis Missouri Republican*, March 20, 1850.

41. Perkins, *Gold Rush Diary*, p. 49.

42. Mrs. Matthew P. Deady, "Diary of Mrs. Matthew P. Deady," *Transactions, Oregon Pioneer Association*, 56th annual reunion (Portland, 1928), p. 59.

43. Decker, *Diaries*, p. 63.

44. Perkins, *Gold Rush Diary*, pp. 9, 23.

45. Carson C. Masiker, "The Linchpin Wagon," *Transactions, Oregon Pioneer Association*, 43d annual reunion (Portland, 1915), p. 207.

46. Walton, *Wagon Days with Mother Walton*, p. 10.

47. John Steele, *Across the Plains* (Chicago: N.p., 1930), p. 110; printed for the Caxton Club.

48. Samuel Eliot Morison, *The Oxford History of the American People* (New York: Oxford University Press, 1965), pp. 546–47.

49. Morgan, ed., *Overland Diary of James A. Pritchard*, p. 55.

50. Peter Burnett, "Recollections of an Old Pioneer," *Oregon Historical Society Quarterly* 5 (1904): 82.

51. Holmes, ed., *Covered Wagon Women*, 5: 282.

52. Ibid., 7:46, 57, 69, 71; 6:233; 9:78.

53. Myres, ed., *Ho for California*, p. 124.

54. See Merrill J. Mattes, "The Sutler's Store at Fort Laramie," *Annals of Wyoming* 18 (1946): 98–106, for more information on the changing prices at Fort Laramie. See also John D. Unruh, *The Plains Across* (Urbana: University of Illinois Press, 1979), pp. 244–301.

55. Holmes, ed., *Covered Wagon Women*, 3:72.

56. Myres, ed., *Ho for California*, p. 65.

57. Mattes, "Sutler's Store at Fort Laramie," p. 99.

58. Holmes, ed., *Covered Wagon Women*, 2:271.

59. Myres, ed., *Ho for California*, pp. 75–76.

60. Holmes, ed., *Covered Wagon Women*, 8:184. See also Unruh, *Plains Across*, chapter 9, for more information on the trading policies of the Mormons.

CHAPTER 3. ESSENTIAL EQUIPMENT

1. Sandra L. Myres, ed., *Ho for California! Women's Overland Diaries from the Huntington Library* (San Marino, Calif.: Huntington Library, 1980), p. 95.

2. Joel Palmer, *Journal of Travels over the Rocky Mountains* (Cleveland: Arthur H. Clark Company, 1906), p. 259.

3. Lansford Warren Hastings, *The Emigrants' Guide to Oregon and California* (Cincinnati, Ohio: G. Conclin, 1845), pp. 143–44.

4. Mary Rockwood Powers, *A Woman's Overland Journal to California* (Fairfield, Wash.: Ye Galleon Press, 1985), p. 22.

5. John S. Zieber, "Diary of John S. Zieber," *Transactions, Oregon Pioneer Association*, 48th annual reunion (Portland, 1920), p. 303.

6. E. S. McComas, *A Journal of Travel* (Portland, Oreg.: Champoeg Press, 1954), p. 12.

7. Kenneth L. Holmes, ed., *Covered Wagon Women: Diaries and Letters from the Western Trails*, 10 vols. to date (Glendale, Calif.: Arthur H. Clark Company, 1983–), 9:160.

8. Clarence B. Bagley, "Crossing the Plains," *Washington Historical Quarterly* 13: 3 (July 1992): 170.

9. Linda Campbell Franklin, *300 Years of Kitchen Collectibles* (Florence, Ala.: Books Americana), p. 444.

10. Ibid., pp. 425–26.

11. Jeanne H. Watson, "Women's Travails and Triumphs on the Overland Trail," *Overland Journal* 9:4 (Winter 1991): 29.

12. Margaret Coffin, *The History and Folklore of American Country Tinware 1700–1900* (Camden, N.J.: Thomas Nelson and Sons, 1968), p. 44.

13. Charles Gray, *The Overland Journal of Charles Glass Gray* (San Marino, Calif.: Huntington Library, 1976), p. 80.

14. Holmes, ed., *Covered Wagon Women*, 9:95.

15. Ibid., 4:268.

16. Dale L. Morgan, ed., *Overland in 1846*, 2 vols. (Georgetown, Calif.: Talisman Press, 1963), 1:21, 2:735.

17. Ibid., 2:736.

18. Susan P. Angell, "Sketch of Mrs. Susan P. Angell," *Transactions, Oregon Pioneer Association*, 48th annual reunion (Portland, 1920), p. 303.

19. Holmes, ed., *Covered Wagon Women*, 8:141, 9:94.

20. Palmer, *Journal of Travels over the Rocky Mountains*, p. 259.

21. Peter H. Burnett, "Letters of Peter H. Burnett," *Oregon Historical Society Quarterly* 3 (1902): 419.

22. S. H. Taylor, "Oregon Bound in 1853," *Oregon Historical Society Quarterly* 22 (1921): 148.

23. Burnett, "Letters," p. 419.

24. Palmer, *Journal of Travels over the Rocky Mountains*, p. 259.

25. Gray, *Overland Journal*, pp. 9, 38.

26. Samuel Dundass and George Keller, *The Journals of Samuel Rutherford Dundass and George Keller, Crossing the Plains to California in 1849–1850* (Fairfield, Wash.: Ye Galleon Press, 1983), p. 69.

27. Bernard J. Reid, *Overland to California with the Pioneer Line* (Stanford, Calif.: Stanford University Press, 1983), p. 77.

28. John S. Wright and J. Ambrose Wight, eds., *The Prairie Farmer* (Chicago: John S. Wright, 1849), p. 55.

29. Eliza Leslie, *Directions for Cookery* (Philadelphia: Henry C. Baird, 1857), p. 409.

30. Holmes, ed., *Covered Wagon Women*, 2:232, 4:65.

31. E. W. Conyers, "Diary of E. W. Conyers," *Transactions, Oregon Pioneer Association*, 33d annual reunion (Portland, 1905), p. 455.

32. Holmes, ed., *Covered Wagon Women*, 5:92.

33. J. Robert Brown, *Diary of J. Robert Brown* (N.p., 1856), p. 13 (photostat copy in Newberry Library, Chicago).

34. Bagley, "Crossing the Plains," p. 170.

35. Elisha Perkins, *Gold Rush Diary: Being the Journal of Elisha Douglass Perkins on the Overland Trail in the Spring and Summer of 1849* (Lexington: University of Kentucky Press, 1967), p. 22.

36. Holmes, ed., *Covered Wagon Women*, 5:268.

37. Myres, ed., *Ho for California*, p. 173.

38. James Hutchings, *Seeking the Elephant, 1849, James M. Hutchings' Overland Journal* (Glendale, Calif.: Arthur H. Clark Company, 1980), p. 174.

39. Holmes, ed., *Covered Wagon Women*, 8:65.

40. Conyers, "Diary of E. W. Conyers," p. 457.

41. Holmes, ed., *Covered Wagon Women*, 2:139, 6:108, 5:110.

42. Gray, *Overland Journal*, p. 14.

43. Holmes, ed., *Covered Wagon Women*, 6:240.

44. Taylor, "Oregon Bound in 1853," p. 149.

45. Holmes, ed., *Covered Wagon Women*, 3:79, 2:228.

46. Reid, *Overland to California with the Pioneer Line*, p. 86.

47. Dale L. Morgan, ed., *The Overland Diary of James A. Pritchard* (Denver: Old West Publishing Company, 1959), p. 154n.44.

48. Richard Barksdale Harwell, *The Mint Julep* (Charlottesville: University Press of Virginia, 1975), p. 30.

49. Eleanor Allen, *Canvas Caravans* (Portland, Oreg.: Binfords and Mort, 1946), p. 57.

50. Gray, *Overland Journal*, p. 48.

51. Basil N. Longsworth, *The Diary of Basil N. Longsworth* (Portland, Oreg.: Historical Records Survey, 1938), p. 33 (transcription).

52. Holmes, ed., *Covered Wagon Women*, 5:282, 6:104, 5:91.

53. John Charles Frémont, *Report of the Exploring Expedi-*

tion to the Rocky Mountains in the Year 1842 (Washington, D.C.: Blair and Rives Printers, 1845), p. 135.

54. Mrs. E. A. Howland, *The New England Economical Housekeeper* (1845; reprint, South Yarmouth, Mass.: Allen D. Bragdon, 1987), p. 32.

55. Allen, *Canvas Caravans*, p. 65.

56. Henry Allyn, "Journal of 1853," *Transactions, Oregon Pioneer Association*, 49th annual reunion (Portland, 1921), p. 414.

57. Holmes, ed., *Covered Wagon Women*, 3:279.

58. Jesse Harritt, "Diary of Jesse Harritt," *Transactions, Oregon Pioneer Association*, 39th annual reunion (Portland, 1911), p. 519.

59. Myres, ed., *Ho for California*, pp. 78, 77.

60. Lillian Schlissel, *Women's Diaries of the Westward Journey* (New York: Schocken Books, 1982), p. 80.

61. Myres, ed., *Ho for California*, p. 104.

62. Holmes, ed., *Covered Wagon Women*, 8:158.

63. Morgan, ed., *Overland in 1846*, 2:565.

64. Conyers, "Diary of E. W. Conyers," p. 441.

65. Myres, ed., *Ho for California*, p. 119.

66. T. C. Elliott, ed., *The Coming of the White Women, 1836* (Portland: Oregon Historical Society, 1937), p. 3.

67. Holmes, ed., *Covered Wagon Women*, 3:66.

68. Myres, ed., *Ho for California*, p. 111.

69. Frémont, *Report*, p. 49.

70. Holmes, ed., *Covered Wagon Women*, 3:74.

71. Myres, ed., *Ho for California*, p. 136.

72. Holmes, ed., *Covered Wagon Women*, 8:51.

73. Tyôzaburô Tanaka, *Tanaka's Cyclopedia of Edible Plants of the World* (Tokyo: Keigashu Publishing Company, 1976), p. 62.

74. Frémont, *Report*, p. 49.

75. Holmes, ed., *Covered Wagon Women*, 1:127, 3:74.

76. Edwin Bryant, *What I Saw in California* (New York: D. Appleton and Company, 1849), p. 122.

77. Holmes, ed., *Covered Wagon Women*, 3:77, 111.

78. Reuben Cole Shaw, *Across the Plains in Forty-Nine* (1896; reprint, Chicago: Lakeside Press, 1948), p. 37.

79. Lodisa Frizzell, *Across the Plains to California in 1852* (New York: New York Public Library, 1915), p. 21.

80. Charles Ross Parke, *Dreams to Dust, A Diary of the California Gold Rush, 1849–1850* (Lincoln: University of Nebraska Press, 1989), p. 16.

81. Holmes, ed., *Covered Wagon Women*, 8:36.

82. Palmer, *Journal of Travels over the Rocky Mountains*, p. 259.

83. *Told by the Pioneers*, vol. 2 (Olympia Wash.: Works Project Administration, 1937), p. 96.

84. Gary Fuller Reese, *The Terriblest Route of All* (Tacoma, Wash.: Tacoma Public Library, 1984), p. 14.

85. Holmes, ed., *Covered Wagon Women*, 9:99–100.

86. Taylor, "Oregon Bound in 1853," pp. 142, 148.

87. J. Leander Bishop, *A History of American Manufactures from 1608 to 1860*, 2 vols. (Philadelphia: Edward Young and Company, 1864), 2:623–24.

88. Tammis Groft, *Cast with Style, Nineteenth Century Cast-Iron Stoves from the Albany Area* (Albany, N.Y.: Albany Institute of History and Art, 1984), p. 15.

89. Josephine Peirce, *Fire on the Hearth* (Springfield, Mass.: Pond-Exkberg Company, 1951), pp. 147, 155.

90. Holmes, ed., *Covered Wagon Women*, 4:257–58.

91. Frizzell, *Across the Plains to California in 1852*, p. 15.

92. Holmes, ed., *Covered Wagon Women*, 9:124.

93. David De Wolf, "Diary of the Overland Trail, 1849, and Letters, 1849–1850, of Captain David De Wolf," *Transactions of the Illinois State Historical Society* (Springfield: Illinois State Historical Library, 1926), p. 191.

94. Holmes, ed., *Covered Wagon Women*, 2:97.

95. Schlissel, *Women's Diaries of the Westward Journey*, p. 168.

96. James Hewitt, *Eye-Witness to Wagon Trains West* (New York: Charles Scribner's Sons, 1973), p. 50.

97. Violet Coe Mumford and the Royal Family Association, *The Royal Way West*, 2 vols. (Baltimore: Gateway Press, 1988), 2:70.

CHAPTER 4. THE WAY THEY COOKED

1. Charlotte Stearns Pengra, *Diary of Mrs. Bynon J. Pengra* (1853; reprint, Eugene, Oreg.: Lane County Pioneer Historical Society, 1959), p. 11.

2. Lillian Schlissel, *Women's Diaries of the Westward Journey* (New York: Schocken Books, 1982), p. 180.

3. Kenneth L. Holmes, ed., *Covered Wagon Women: Diaries and Letters from the Western Trails*, 10 vols. to date (Glendale, Calif.: Arthur H. Clark Company, 1983–), 8:39, 54; 5:154, 125.

4. Peter Decker, *The Diaries of Peter Decker* (Georgetown, Calif.: Talisman Press, 1966), pp. 69, 75.

5. Dale L. Morgan, ed., *Overland in 1846*, 2 vols. (Georgetown, Calif.: Talisman Press, 1963), 2:540, 553.

6. John Charles Frémont, *Report of the Exploring Expedition to the Rocky Mountains in the Year 1842* (Washington, D.C.: Blair and Rives Printers, 1845), pp. 21–22.

7. Reubin Gold Thwaites, ed., *Original Journals of the Lewis and Clark Expeditions, 1804–1806* (New York: Dodd, Mead and Company, 1904), pp. 15–16.

8. Sandra L. Myres, ed., *Ho for California! Women's Overland Diaries from the Huntington Library* (San Marino, Calif.: Huntington Library, 1980), p. 119.

9. Decker, *Diaries*, p. 277n.111.

10. Holmes, ed., *Covered Wagon Women*, 4:290, 1:237.

11. Hyla M. Clark, *The Tin Can Book* (New York: New American Library, 1977), p. 14.

12. Holmes, ed., *Covered Wagon Women*, 8:68.

13. Frederick Young, ed., "Jason Lee Diary," *Oregon Historical Quarterly* 17 (1916): 254.

14. Holmes, ed., *Covered Wagon Women*, 5:246, 15–16.

15. Elisha Perkins, *Gold Rush Diary: Being the Journal of Elisha Douglass Perkins on the Overland Trail in the Spring and Summer of 1849* (Lexington: University of Kentucky Press, 1967), p. 176.

16. *Told by the Pioneers*, vol. 2 (Olympia, Wash.: Works Project Administration, 1938), p. 75.

17. Peter H. Burnett, "Letters of Peter H. Burnett," *Oregon Historical Society Quarterly* 3 (1902): 419.

18. Holmes, ed., *Covered Wagon Women*, 6:236.

19. Ibid., p. 195.

20. Solomon N. Carvalho, *Incidents of Travel and Adventure in the Far West* (Philadelphia: Jewish Publications Society of America, 1954), pp. 148–49.

21. Samuel Dundass and George Keller, *The Journals of*

Samuel Rutherford Dundass and George Keller, Crossing the Plains to California in 1849–1850 (Fairfield, Wash.: Ye Galleon Press, 1983), pp. 78, 87.

22. Alonzo Delano, *Life on the Plains and among the Diggings* (Auburn, N. Y.: Miller, Orton and Mulligan, 1854), p. 44.

23. Holmes, ed., *Covered Wagon Women*, 8:182, 3:260.

24. Decker, *Diaries*, pp. 67, 55.

25. Holmes, ed., *Covered Wagon Women*, 5:220.

26. Edwin Bryant, *What I Saw in California* (New York: D. Appleton, 1849), p. 35.

27. John S. Zieber, "Diary of John S. Zieber," *Transactions, Oregon Pioneer Association*, 48th annual reunion (Portland, 1920), p. 307.

28. Holmes, ed., *Covered Wagon Women*, 6:198.

29. George Vancouver, *Voyage of Discovery to the North Pacific Ocean and Round the World*, 3 vols. (1798; reprint, New York: Da Capo Press, 1967), 1:249.

30. Morgan, ed., *Overland in 1846*, 2:554.

31. Joseph W. Ware, *The Emigrants' Guide to California* (1849; reprint, New York: Da Capo Press, 1972), p. 15.

32. Bryant, *What I Saw in California*, p. 59.

33. Holmes, ed., *Covered Wagon Women*, 4:90.

34. Myres, ed., *Ho for California*, p. 61.

35. Inez E. Parker, "Early Recollections of an Oregon Pioneer," *Transactions, Oregon Pioneer Association*, 56th annual reunion (Portland, 1928), p. 18.

36. Mary Rockwood Powers, *A Woman's Overland Journal to California* (Fairfield, Wash.: Ye Galleon Press, 1985), p. 53.

37. Holmes, ed., *Covered Wagon Women*, 6:244–45.

38. Marcia Byrom Hartwell, ed., *A Sampler of Recipes 1796 to 1908* (Northampton, Mass.: privately published, 1984), p. 61.

39. Holmes, ed., *Covered Wagon Women*, 4:268.

40. Lettice Bryan, *The Kentucky Housewife* (1839; reprint, Columbia: University of South Carolina Press, 1991), pp. 250–51.

41. Sarah J. Hale, *Mrs. Hale's New Cookbook* (Philadelphia: T. B. Peterson and Brothers, 1857), p. 335.

42. Holmes, ed., *Covered Wagon Women*, 4:65, 268.

43. Madeline Angell, *A Field Guide to Berries and Berry-*

like Fruits (Indianapolis: Bobbs-Merrill Company, 1981), pp. 37, 146.

44. William Weaver, ed., *A Quaker Woman's Cookbook* (1853; reprint, Philadelphia: University of Pennsylvania Press, 1982), p. 88.

45. Bryan, *Kentucky Housewife*, p. 395.

46. Holmes, ed., *Covered Wagon Women*, 2:226.

47. Ibid., 3:41–42, 5:134.

48. Schlissel, *Women's Diaries of the Westward Journey*, pp. 169–70.

49. Virginia Wilcox Ivinsa, *Pen Pictures of Early Western Days* (N.p., 1905), p. 68.

50. Charles Ross Parke, *Dreams to Dust, A Diary of the California Gold Rush, 1849–1850* (Lincoln: University of Nebraska Press, 1989), p. 6.

51. Perkins, *Gold Rush Diary*, p. 72.

52. Clifford Drury, ed., *First White Women over the Rockies* (Glendale, Calif.: Arthur H. Clarke Company, 1963), p. 78.

53. Josiah T. Marshall, *The Farmer's and Emigrant's Handbook* (Cincinnati, Ohio: Applegate and Company, 1855), p. 128.

54. Holmes, ed., *Covered Wagon Women*, 1:195.

55. Phoebe Goodell Judson, *A Pioneer's Search for the Ideal Home* (Bellingham, Wash.: Union Printing, Binding, and Stationary Company, 1925), pp. 66–67, 36–37.

56. Bryan, *Kentucky Housewife*, p. 320.

57. Edith Beebe Carhart, *A History of Bellingham* (Bellingham, Wash.: Argonaut Press, 1926), p. 38.

58. Holmes, ed., *Covered Wagon Women*, 4:268.

59. Weaver, ed., *Quaker Woman's Cookbook*, p. xix.

60. Lodisa Frizzell, *Across the Plains to California in 1852* (New York: New York Public Library, 1915), p. 20.

61. James M. Hutchings, *Seeking the Elephant, 1849, James M. Hutchings' Overland Journal* (Glendale, Calif.: Arthur H. Clark Company, 1980), p. 137.

62. Evan Jones, *American Food, the Gastronomic Story* (New York: E. P. Dutton and Company, 1975), p. 75n.5.

63. *American Agriculturist* 6 (November 1847): 347.

64. *The Ladies' Aid Society First M. E. Church Cook Book* (Seattle, Wash.: Covington and Jordan, 1906), p. 49.

65. Holmes, ed., *Covered Wagon Women*, 4:63.

66. Hartwell, ed., *Sampler of Recipes*, p. 54.

67. Jeanne Watson, ed., *To the Land of Gold and Wickedness: The 1848–1859 Diary of Lorena H. Hays* (St. Louis: Patrice Press, 1988), p. 94, 339n.76.

68. Weaver, ed., *Quaker Woman's Cookbook*, p. ix.

69. Burnett, "Letters," p. 416.

70. Morgan, ed., *Overland in 1846*, 2:612.

71. Holmes, ed., *Covered Wagon Women*, 1:121, 224.

72. Dundass and Keller, *Journals*, p. 21.

73. Perkins, *Gold Rush Diary*, p. 35.

74. Bryant, *What I Saw in California*, p. 96.

75. Schlissel, *Women's Diaries of the Westward Journey*, p. 176.

76. Carvalho, *Incidents of Travel*, pp. 95–96.

77. T. C. Elliott, ed., *The Coming of White Women* (1836; reprint, Portland: Oregon Historical Society, 1937), p. 10.

78. Holmes, ed., *Covered Wagon Women*, 3:135.

79. Charles Glass Gray, *The Overland Journal of Charles Glass Gray* (San Marino, Calif.: Huntington Library, 1976), p. 27.

80. Myres, ed., *Ho for California*, p. 108.

81. William M. Colvig, "Annual Address," *Transactions, Oregon Pioneer Association*, 44th annual reunion (Portland, 1916), p. 339.

82. Schlissel, *Women's Diaries of the Westward Journey*, p. 177.

83. Joel Palmer, *Journal of Travels over the Rocky Mountains* (Cleveland, Ohio: Arthur H. Clark Company, 1906), p. 53.

84. Edward E. Parrish, "Crossing the Plains," *Transactions, Oregon Pioneer Association*, 16th annual reunion (Portland, 1888), p. 93.

85. Lorenzo Sawyer, *Way Sketches Containing Incidents of Travel across the Plains* (New York: Edward Eberstadt, 1926), p. 36.

86. Holmes, ed., *Covered Wagon Women*, 8:127.

87. Carvalho, *Incidents of Travel*, p. 96.

88. Holmes, ed., *Covered Wagon Women*, 9:161.

89. Frizzell, *Across the Plains to California in 1852*, p. 24.

90. Holmes, ed., *Covered Wagon Women*, 4:107.

91. Hutchings, *Seeking the Elephant*, pp. 169, 96.

92. Eleanor Allen, *Canvas Caravans* (Portland, Oreg.: Binfords and Mort, 1946), p. 69.

93. Holmes, ed., *Covered Wagon Women*, 4:102–3, 6:248.

94. John Unruh, *The Plains Across* (Urbana: University of Illinois Press, 1979), p. 165.

95. Holmes, ed., *Covered Wagon Women*, 8:158, 2:266, 3:74, 4:102.

96. Gray, *Overland Journal*, p. 70.

97. Perkins, *Gold Rush Diary*, p. 76, 85.

98. Holmes, ed., *Covered Wagon Women*, 3:79, 6:236–37.

99. Schlissel, *Women's Diaries of the Westward Journey*, p. 221.

100. John Faragher, *Women and Men on the Overland Trail* (New Haven, Conn.: Yale University Press, 1979), p. 138.

101. From Elizabeth Duncan, *California Trail Diary*, transcribed from the original by Katie Armitage (1867; manuscript, University of Kansas Special Collections, Lawrence).

102. Holmes, ed., *Covered Wagon Women*, 4:89, 7:67.

103. Elizabeth Page, *Wagons West* (New York: Farrar and Rinehart, 1930), p. 115.

104. Holmes, ed., *Covered Wagon Women*, 5:40, 95.

105. Elliott, ed., *Coming of White Women*, pp. 5, 6.

106. Perkins, *Gold Rush Diary*, p. 4.

107. Holmes, ed., *Covered Wagon Women*, 3:186, 8:39.

108. Ibid., 8:53.

CHAPTER 5. THE GLORIOUS FOURTH

1. Kenneth L. Holmes, ed., *Covered Wagon Women: Diaries and Letters from the Western Trails*, 10 vols. to date (Glendale, Calif.: Arthur H. Clark Company, 1983–), 6:166.

2. Robert Pettus Hay, "Frontier Patriotism, on Parade: Westward the Glorious Fourth of July," *Journal of the West* 5:3 (July 1966): 313.

3. Charles W. Martin and Charles W. Martin, Jr., "The Fourth of July: A Holiday on the Trail," *Overland Journal* 10:2 (Summer 1992): 3.

4. Merrill J. Mattes, *The Great Platte River Road* (1969; reprint, Lincoln: University of Nebraska Press, 1989), p. 380.

5. Peter Decker, *The Diaries of Peter Decker: Overland to California in 1849* (Georgetown, Calif.: Talisman Press, 1966), p. 93.

6. Elisha Perkins, *Gold Rush Diary: Being the Journal of Elisha Douglass Perkins on the Overland Trail in the Spring and Summer of 1849* (Lexington: University of Kentucky Press, 1967), p. 66.

7. Diana Carter Applebaum, *The Glorious Fourth* (New York: Facts on File, 1989), p. 6.

8. See ibid., pp. 1–33, for a discussion of early Fourth of July celebrations.

9. Holmes, ed., *Covered Wagon Women*, 2:111, 8:144–45.

10. Lettice Bryan, *The Kentucky Housewife* (1838; reprint, Columbia: University of South Carolina Press, 1991), p. 308.

11. Sandra L. Myres, ed., *Ho for California! Women's Overland Diaries from the Huntington Library* (San Marino, Calif.: Huntington Library, 1980), pp. 127–28.

12. Margaret Visser, *Much Depends on Dinner* (New York: Grove Press, 1986), p. 45.

13. J. Leander Bishop, *A History of American Manufactures 1608 to 1860*, 3 vols. (1868; reprint, New York: Augustus M. Kelley, 1966), 3:161–62.

14. J. S. Holliday, "On the Gold Rush Trail,": *American West* 5:4 (July 1968): 38.

15. Janice B. Longone, *Mother Maize and King Corn* (Ann Arbor, Mich.: William L. Clements Library, 1986), p. 20.

16. John Charles Frémont, *The Exploring Expedition to the Rocky Mountains, Oregon and California* (Auburn, N.Y.: Derby and Miller, 1854), p. 28.

17. Jeanne H. Watson, "Women's Travails and Triumphs on the Overland Trail," *Overland Journal* 9:4 (Winter 1991): 29.

18. Phoebe Goodell Judson, *A Pioneer's Search for an Ideal Home* (Bellingham, Wash.: Union Printing, Binding, and Stationary Company, 1925), p. 43.

19. Holliday, "On the Gold Rush Trail," p. 38.

20. Susan Walton, *Wagon Days with Mother Walton* (1931; manuscript, University of Washington Special Collections, Seattle): p. 72.

21. Violet Coe Mumford and the Royal Family Association, 2 vols. (Baltimore: Gateway Press, 1988), 2:72.

22. Sarah J. Hale, *Mrs. Hale's New Cookbook* (Philadelphia: T. B. Peterson and Brothers, 1857), p. 400.

23. Mary L. Williams, ed., *An Army Wife's Cookbook* (Tucson, Ariz.: Southwest Parks and Monuments Association, 1972), p. 43.

24. *The Ladies' Aid Society First M. E. Church Cook Book* (Seattle, Wash.: Covington and Jordan, 1906), pp. 53, 55.

25. Charles Ross Parke, *Dreams to Dust, A Diary of the California Gold Rush, 1849–1850* (Lincoln: University of Nebraska Press, 1989), p. 46.

26. E. W. Conyers, "Diary of E. W. Conyers," *Transactions, Oregon Pioneer Association*, 33d annual reunion (Portland, 1905), p. 458.

27. Ibid., pp. 457–58.

28. Holmes, ed., *Covered Wagon Women*, 3:36, 4:103.

29. Bryan, *Kentucky Housewife*, p. 178.

30. Matthew Field, *Prairie and Mountain Sketches*, ed. Kate L. Gregg and John Francis McDermott (Norman: University of Oklahoma Press, 1957), pp. 67, 68.

31. Holmes, ed., *Covered Wagon Women*, 5:229.

32. Samuel Dundass and George Keller, *The Journals of Samuel Dundass and George Keller, Crossing the Plains to California in 1849–1850* (Fairfield, Wash.: Ye Galleon Press, 1983), p. 30.

33. Judson, *Pioneer's Search for an Ideal Home*, p. 43.

34. Holmes, ed., *Covered Wagon Women*, 4:103.

35. Martin and Martin, Jr., "Fourth of July," p. 12.

36. Waverly Root, *Food* (New York: Simon and Schuster, 1980), p. 512.

37. Charles S. Bragdon, *Metal Decorating from Start to Finishes* (Freeport, Maine: Bond Wheelwright Company, 1961), p. 83.

38. Martin and Martin, Jr., "Fourth of July," p. 12.

39. Dundass and Keller, *Journals*, p. 88.

40. Martin and Martin, Jr., "Fourth of July," p. 11.

41. Field, *Prairie and Mountain Sketches*, p. 71.

42. O. B. Sperlin, "Earliest Celebrations of Independence Day," *Pacific Northwest Quarterly* 35:3 (July 1944): 219.

43. Dale L. Morgan, ed., *Overland in 1846*, 2 vols. (Georgetown, Calif.: Talisman Press, 1963), 2:586.

44. Conyers, "Diary," p. 457.
45. Holmes, ed., *Covered Wagon Women*, 1:73.

EPILOGUE

1. Kenneth L. Holmes, ed., *Covered Wagon Women: Diaries and Letters from the Western Trails*, 10 vols. to date (Glendale, Calif.: Arthur H. Clark Company, 1983–), 5:133–34, 248; see also John D. Unruh, *The Plains Across* (Urbana: University of Illinois Press, 1979), pp. 338–78 for a discussion of West Coast assistance to the emigrants.

2. *Told by the Pioneers*, 3 vols. (Olympia, Wash.: Works Project Administration, 1937), 3:175.

3. Ibid., 2:112.

SUGGESTIONS FOR
FURTHER READING

I have based my research on the numerous diaries and letters that give extensive detail about this unique period of American history. I would call particular attention to the ten volumes of *Covered Wagon Women* by Kenneth Holmes, *Overland in 1846*, edited by Dale Morgan, and Lillian Schlissel's *Women's Diaries of the Westward Journey*. In addition to offering a sample of excellent diaries and letters, these books provide a vast amount of data about persons and places important in the westward movement.

For people who want to know more about the Oregon-California Trail, there is supplementary material, in addition to the sources cited in the notes. First are several general histories, accounts of journeys, and indexes to additional diaries. Second are a number of books concerned with culinary history and recipes from the past. Third, although I have treated the contributions of both men and women in the long trip across the plains and prairies, this trip dramatically illustrated the role of brave and resourceful women, the final category of additional references.

GENERAL HISTORIES, DIARIES, AND INDEXES

Armitage, Susan. *Women and Western American History*. Wellesley, Mass.: Wellesley College Center for Research on Women, 1984.

Armitage, Susan, et al. *Women in the West: A Guide to Manuscript Sources*. New York: Garland Publishing, 1991.

Bidwell, John. *A Journey to California, with Observations about the Country, Climate, and Route to This Country*. San Francisco: J. H. Nash, 1937.

Hafen, LeRoy R., and Ann W. Hafen. *Handcarts to Zion: The Story of a Unique Western Migration, 1856–1860*. Glendale, Calif.: Arthur C. Clark Company, 1992; paperback, Lincoln: University of Nebraska Press, 1992.

Herndon, Sarah R. *Days on the Road: Crossing the Plains in 1865*. New York: Burr Printing House, 1902.

Larkin, Jack. *The Reshaping of Everyday Life, 1790–1840*. New York: Harper Collins, 1989.

Mattes, Merrill J. *Platte River Road Narratives: A Descriptive Bibliography of Travel over the Great Central Overland Route to Oregon, California, Utah, Colorado, Montana, and other Western States and Territories, 1812–1866*. Urbana: University of Illinois Press, 1988.

Meeker, Ezra. *The Ox Team; or The Old Oregon Trail, 1852–1906: An Account of the Author's Trip across the Plains, from the Missouri River to Puget Sound*. Omaha, Nebr.: By the author, 1906.

Paden, Irene. *The Wake of the Prairie Schooner*. Tucson, Ariz.: Patrice Press, 1983.

Read, George Willis. *A Pioneer of 1850: The Record of a Journey Overland from Independence, Missouri, to Hangtown (Placerville), California, in the Spring of 1850*. Georgia Willis Read, ed. Boston: Little, Brown and Company, 1927.

Royce, Sarah. *A Frontier Lady: Recollections of the Gold Rush and Early California*. New Haven, Conn.: Yale University Press, 1932; reprint, Lincoln: University of Nebraska Press, 1977.

Rumer, Thomas A. *The Wagon Trains of 'Forty-Four: A Comparative View of the Individual Caravans in the Emigration of 1844 to Oregon*. Spokane, Wash.: Arthur C. Clark Company, 1991.

Sanford, Mollie D. *Mollie: Journal of Mollie Dorsey Sanford in Nebraska and Colorado Territories, 1857–1866*. Lincoln: University of Nebraska Press, 1959.

Stewart, George R. *The California Trail: An Epic with Many Heroes*. New York: McGraw-Hill, 1962; reprint, Lincoln: University of Nebraska Press, 1983.

Townley, John. *The Trail West: A Bibliography-Index to Western American Trails, 1841–1869*. Reno, Nev.: Jamison Station, 1988.

Ward, Dillis B. *Across the Plains in Eighteen Fifty-Three*. Wenatchee, Wash.: World Publishing Company, 1945; reprint, Seattle: Shorey, 1983.

CULINARY HISTORY

The American Heritage Cookbook, by the editors of *American Heritage*. Historical foods consultant, Helen D. Bullock. New York: American Heritage Publishing Company, 1964; reprint, 1980.

Arnott, Margaret. *Gastronomy: The Anthropology of Food and Food Habits*. The Hague: Mouton, 1975; distributed in the United States and Canada, Chicago: Aldine, 1975.

Carpenter, Kenneth J. *The History of Scurvy and Vitamin C*. Cambridge: Cambridge University Press, 1986.

Child, Lydia M. *The American Frugal Housewife*. Boston: Carter, Hendee and Company, 1835; reprint, Ohio State University Library, 1971.

Coffin, Margaret. *The History and Folklore of American Country Tinware, 1700–1900*. Camden, N.J.: Thomas Nelson and Sons, 1968; reprint, New York: Galahad Books, 1974.

Hooker, Richard J. *Food and Drink in America: A History*. Indianapolis: Bobbs-Merrill Company, 1981.

Peet, Louise J., et al. *Household Equipment*. 8th ed. New York: John Wiley and Sons, 1934; reprint, 1974.

Root, Waverly, and Richard De Rochemont. *Eating in America*. New York: William Morrow, 1976.

Tannahill, Reay. *Food in History*. New York: Stein and Day, 1973.

Trager, James. *The Enriched, Fortified, Concentrated, Country-fresh, Lip-smacking, Finger-licking, International, Unexpurgated Foodbook*. New York: Grossman Publishers, 1970.

WOMEN'S STUDIES

Armitage, Susan H., and Elizabeth Jameson, eds. *The Women's West*. Norman: University of Oklahoma Press, 1987.

Jeffrey, Julie R. *Frontier Women: The Trans-Mississippi West, 1840–1880*. New York: Hill and Wang, 1979.

Levy, JoAnn. *They Saw the Elephant: Women in the California Gold Rush*. Harnden, Conn.: Shoestring, 1990; reprint, Lincoln: University of Nebraska Press, 1992.

Lockley, Fred. *The Lockley Files, Volume 1: Conversations with Pioneer Women*. Eugene, Oreg.: Rainy Day Press, 1981.

Moynihan, Ruth B., et al., eds. *So Much to Be Done: Women Settlers* on the Mining and Ranching Frontier. Lincoln: University of Nebraska Press, 1990.

Riley, Glenda. The Female Frontier: A Comparative View of Women on the Prairie and Plains. Lawrence: University Press of Kansas, 1988.

————. Women and Indians on the Frontier, 1825–1915. Albuquerque: University of New Mexico Press, 1984.

Schlissel, Lillian, et al. Far from Home: Families of the Westward Journey. New York: Schocken Books, 1989.

INDEX

INDEX